Fischer and Bloomfield's text is timely, comprehensive, and highly accessible to practitioners, trainers, researchers, and educational decision-makers. It covers a wealth of issues associated with school teleconsultation—from building rapport to mitigating barriers—with the breadth and depth needed to gain expertise on a highly relevant topic. It is a must-have for all service providers in this new age of telecommunications.
—**Susan M. Sheridan, PhD,** Director, Nebraska Center for Research on Children, Youth, Families and Schools, University of Nebraska-Lincoln

Teleconsultation is the next frontier of school consultation and there is a clear need for a guide that expertly informs its practice. This volume by Drs. Fischer and Bloomfield is exactly that guide. By effectively combining theory and research, *Teleconsultation in Schools: A Guide to Collaborative Practice* provides a wealth of useful practice suggestions and is highly recommended.
—**William P. Erchul, PhD, ABPP,** Professor Emeritus of Psychology, North Carolina State University, Raleigh

Teleconsultation in Schools: A Guide to Collaborative Practice by Fischer and Bloomfield is a groundbreaking text. The authors provide compelling arguments for how technology can be used to increase mental health interventions in clinical and applied educational settings. The book features foundations of teleconsultation, guidelines for consultation within school settings, and ways to overcome barriers as well as directions for future work. All this content is based on experience in research and practice. This is a most compelling book for psychologists and other professionals interested in expanding interventions in their practice.
—**Thomas Kratochwill, PhD,** Professor of School Psychology, Wisconsin Center for Education Research, School of Education, University of Wisconsin–Madison

Teleconsultation in Schools

Applying Psychology in the Schools Book Series

Assessing Bilingual Children in Context: An Integrated Approach
    Edited by Amanda B. Clinton

Autism Spectrum Disorder in Children and Adolescents: Evidence-Based Assessment and Intervention in Schools
    Edited by Lee A. Wilkinson

Behavioral Interventions in Schools: Evidence-Based Positive Strategies, Second Edition
    Edited by Steven G. Little and Angeleque Akin-Little

Empowered Families, Successful Children: Early Intervention Programs That Work
    Susan Epps and Barbara J. Jackson

Empowered Learning in Secondary Schools: Promoting Positive Youth Development Through a Multitiered System of Supports
    Cynthia E. Hazel

Enhancing Relationships Between Children and Teachers
    Robert C. Pianta

Health-Related Disorders in Children and Adolescents: A Guidebook for Educators and Service Providers, Second Edition
    Edited by Michelle M. Perfect, Cynthia A. Riccio, and Melissa A. Bray

Healthy Eating in Schools: Evidence-Based Interventions to Help Kids Thrive
    Catherine P. Cook-Cottone, Evelyn Tribole, and Tracy L. Tylka

Implementation of Mental Health Programs in Schools: A Change Agent's Guide
    Susan G. Forman

Promoting Mind–Body Health in Schools: Interventions for Mental Health Professionals
    Edited by Cheryl Maykel and Melissa A. Bray

Psychoeducational Assessment and Intervention for Ethnic Minority Children: Evidence-Based Approaches
    Edited by Scott L. Graves Jr. and Jamilia J. Blake

School-Based Mental Health Services: Creating Comprehensive and Culturally Specific Programs
   Bonnie Kaul Nastasi, Rachel Bernstein Moore, and Kristen M. Varjas

School-Centered Interventions: Evidence-Based Strategies for Social, Emotional, and Academic Success
   Dennis J. Simon

Self-Regulated Learning Interventions With At-Risk Youth: Enhancing Adaptability, Performance, and Well-Being
   Edited by Timothy J. Cleary

Single-Case Intervention Research: Methodological and Statistical Advances
   Edited by Thomas R. Kratochwill and Joel R. Levin

Teleconsultation in Schools: A Guide to Collaborative Practice
   Aaron J. Fischer and Bradley S. Bloomfield

Testing Accommodations for Students With Disabilities: Research-Based Practice
   Benjamin J. Lovett and Lawrence J. Lewandowski

Treatment Integrity: A Foundation for Evidence-Based Practice in Applied Psychology
   Edited by Lisa M. Hagermoser Sanetti and Thomas R. Kratochwill

Universal Screening in Educational Settings: Evidence-Based Decision Making for Schools
   Edited by Ryan J. Kettler, Todd A. Glover, Craig A. Albers, and Kelly A. Feeney-Kettler

Working With Parents of Aggressive Children: A Practitioner's Guide, Second Edition
   Timothy A. Cavell and Lauren B. Quetsch

Working With Parents of Noncompliant Children: A Guide to Evidence-Based Parent Training for Practitioners and Students
   Mark D. Shriver and Keith D. Allen

Teleconsultation in Schools A Guide to Collaborative Practice

Aaron J. Fischer and Bradley S. Bloomfield

 AMERICAN PSYCHOLOGICAL ASSOCIATION

Copyright © 2024 by the American Psychological Association. All rights reserved. Except as permitted under the United States Copyright Act of 1976, no part of this publication may be reproduced or distributed in any form or by any means, including, but not limited to, the process of scanning and digitization, or stored in a database or retrieval system, without the prior written permission of the publisher.

The opinions and statements published are the responsibility of the authors, and such opinions and statements do not necessarily represent the policies of the American Psychological Association.

Published by
American Psychological Association
750 First Street, NE
Washington, DC 20002
https://www.apa.org

Order Department
https://www.apa.org/pubs/books
order@apa.org

Typeset in Charter and Interstate by Circle Graphics, Inc., Reisterstown, MD

Printer: Gasch Printing, Odenton, MD
Cover Designer: Gwen J. Grafft, Minneapolis, MN

Library of Congress Cataloging-in-Publication Data

Names: Fischer, Aaron J., author. | Bloomfield, Bradley S., author.
Title: Teleconsultation in schools : a guide to collaborative practice / Aaron J. Fischer and Bradley S. Bloomfield.
Description: Washington, DC : American Psychological Association, [2024] | Series: Applying psychology in the schools book series | Includes bibliographical references and index.
Identifiers: LCCN 2023010275 (print) | LCCN 2023010276 (ebook) | ISBN 9781433839092 (paperback) | ISBN 9781433839108 (ebook)
Subjects: LCSH: School psychologists--Training of--Effect of technological innovations on. | School psychology--Technological innovations. | Educational technology. | Telecommunication in education. | BISAC: PSYCHOLOGY / Psychotherapy / Counseling | PSYCHOLOGY / Developmental / Adolescent
Classification: LCC LB1027.55 .F573 2024 (print) | LCC LB1027.55 (ebook) | DDC 371.7/13--dc23/eng/20230621
LC record available at https://lccn.loc.gov/2023010275
LC ebook record available at https://lccn.loc.gov/2023010276

https://doi.org/10.1037/0000366-000

Printed in the United States of America

10 9 8 7 6 5 4 3 2 1

Contents

List of Tables and Figures	*ix*
Series Foreword—Michelle Perfect	*xi*
Preface	*xiii*
I. FOUNDATIONS OF SCHOOL TELECONSULTATION	**1**
1. The Historical Context of School Teleconsultation	9
2. Professional and Ethical Issues in School Teleconsultation	23
II. A PRACTICAL GUIDE TO SCHOOL TELECONSULTATION	**33**
3. Relationship Building During School Teleconsultation	43
4. Problem Identification During School Teleconsultation	71
5. Problem Analysis During School Teleconsultation	87
6. Intervention Planning, Training, and Support	103
7. Evaluation of the School Teleconsultation Process and Outcomes	121
III. BARRIERS TO SCHOOL TELECONSULTATION AND FUTURE DIRECTIONS	**131**
8. Navigating Barriers to School Teleconsultation	135
9. Future Directions in School Teleconsultation	147
References	*161*
Index	*175*
About the Authors	*181*

List of Tables and Figures

I. FOUNDATIONS OF SCHOOL TELECONSULTATION — 1
Figure PI.1 The School Teleconsultation Process — 4
Figure PI.2 Levels of Support in School Teleconsultation — 5
Table PI.1 Key Terms — 6

II. A PRACTICAL GUIDE TO SCHOOL TELECONSULTATION — 33
Table PII.1 Problem-Solving Teleconsultation Overview — 36
Table 3.1 Example Responsibility Allocation Sheet — 56
Table 3.2 Opportunities to Respond — 58
Table 3.3 Strategies and Tools to Increase Rapport — 58
Table 3.4 Strategies to Address Interpersonal Considerations During Teleconsultation — 65
Table 4.1 Antecedents and Consequences — 74
Table 4.2 Setting Events — 75
Table 4.3 Data Collection Methods and Applications — 76
Table 4.4 Data Sources for Functional Behavior Assessments (FBAs) — 79
Figure 5.1 Example Bar Graph: Frequency of Target Behavior — 89
Figure 5.2 Example Line Graph: Rate of Behavior Incidents by Activity Type — 90
Figure 5.3 Rate of Property Destruction Across Sessions — 100
Table 6.1 Strategies by Behavioral Function — 105
Exhibit 6.1 Suggested Texts for Behavior Supports in Schools — 105

Table 6.2 Ways to Provide Performance Feedback and Suggested
Circumstances to Use the Performance Feedback Method   112

Table 7.1 Example Measures for the Assessment of Social Validity   122

III. BARRIERS TO SCHOOL TELECONSULTATION AND FUTURE DIRECTIONS   131

Table 8.1 Technical Considerations Impacting Rapport During Teleconsultation and Mitigation Strategies for Effective Rapport Building and Maintenance   140

Series Foreword

Outside of their homes, children spend more time in schools than in any other setting. From gun violence tragedies such as Uvalde, Parkland, and Sandy Hook to more hopeful developments such as the movement toward improved mental and physical health and academic achievement, there is an ongoing need for high-quality writing that speaks to ways in which children, families, and communities associated with schools worldwide can be supported through the application of sound psychological research, theory, and practice.

The American Psychological Association (APA) Books Program and APA Division 16 (School Psychology) have partnered to produce the Applying Psychology in the Schools Book Series for over 2 decades. The mission of this series is to increase the visibility of the science, practice, and policy for children and adolescents in schools and communities. The result has been a robust collection of scholarly work that appeals to psychologists and individuals from all fields who have reason to seek and use what psychology has to offer in schools.

Drs. Aaron J. Fischer and Bradley S. Bloomfield, authors of *Teleconsultation in Schools: A Guide to Collaborative Practice*, have provided a tremendous resource for health-service psychologists, particularly school psychologists. Over the past decade, but especially since the COVID-19 pandemic, the need for virtual modalities to deliver school-based psychological services has grown. As technologies are developed, it is critically important for practitioners to have a practical guide on best practices for use of teleconsultation, including the ethical and legal aspects, problem-solving approaches, and challenges to service delivery. The book is filled with practical suggestions, guidance, and resources as the authors detail the process of developing relationships, identifying problems, analyzing the problems, intervention planning, treatment implementation, and evaluation of impact.

Since its initiation, many individuals have made significant contributions to this book series. We would like to acknowledge the dedication of past series editors Sandra L. Christensen, Catherine Christo, Jan Hughes, R. Steve McCallum, David McIntosh, LeAdelle Phelps, Linda Reddy, Susan Sheridan, Christopher H. Skinner, David Shriberg, Melissa Pearrow, and Michelle Perfect. Second, we also thank Linda Malnasi McCarter and the editorial team of APA Books for their work and support, as well as all of the people at APA Books who have worked behind the scenes to bring this book to fruition.

The leadership of Division 16 welcomes your comments about this volume and your ideas for other topics you would like to see explored in this series. To share your thoughts, please visit the Division 16 website (https://www.apa.org/about/division/div16).

—*Michelle Perfect, PhD*
Series Editor

Preface

Since the 1980s, technological innovations have transformed the way people work, socialize, and learn. Technology allows family, friends, coworkers, and clients to seamlessly communicate with each other—live (e.g., videoconferencing, phone calls) or at a time that is convenient for them (e.g., email, text messaging)—from almost anywhere in the world. This has been a tremendous leap forward from a few decades ago, when many of these activities were not even feasible. For many mental and behavioral health practitioners, technology that is ubiquitous with school practice and personal communication can fit in their pocket. Furthermore, applications available on these devices can streamline data collection, storage, analysis, and presentation to support student learning and progress monitoring. In the field of school psychology, these technological developments, paired with contemporary applications of school psychology practice, increase the efficiency, accessibility, and practicality of evidence-based supports.

Teleconsultation, broadly, is the use of these technologies to support behavioral and mental health services, professional development, and supervision, using synchronous and asynchronous means, to meet the specific needs of the clients. Students, educators, caregivers, and school systems can benefit from using teleconsultation in schools, through increased access to knowledge, skills, and support to best meet their learning goals. It is not necessarily one-size-fits-all; rather, individual and contextual factors impact the specific service model, goals, and outcomes.

Teleconsultation in Schools: A Guide to Collaborative Practice is intended to be a primary resource for educating graduate students and guiding school-based professionals. The book is intended to help school consultants use contemporary technology to support and improve professional learning and practice in school teleconsultation. It provides not only an overview of school teleconsultation's historical foundations and important professional and ethical considerations for its practitioners but also a step-by-step procedural guide to teleconsulting practice.

As the authors of this text, we have many people to whom we would like to show our gratitude. First, it was a pleasure working with Dr. Michelle Perfect and folks at the American Psychological Association, including Division 16 (School Psychology), who supported the book from its inception through its publication. We want to recognize the families, educators, and students who participated in early teleconsultation studies to help us understand how we could support individuals from schools across the United States—and, ultimately, internationally. Additionally, we want to thank our colleagues and collaborators who inspired us through their innovative research, amazing conversations about the work, and supportive contributions on teleconsultation projects. Finally, we would like to give our deepest gratitude to Lean Agravante, Marissa Gochnour, and Annie Chuang for their editorial and design support, including the supplemental resources and the images included in the case studies.

Dr. Fischer sincerely thanks all of the students and members of the University of Utah Technology in Training, Education, and Consultation Lab for their tireless effort to improve the lives of students and families across Utah. Most importantly, he thanks his partner, Nina, and his two children, Davi and Zevi, for providing a loving space to connect and grow together during the pandemic and while writing this book.

Dr. Bloomfield would like to thank his colleagues across the world who have influenced this work. He gives a thank you as well to all of his friends and family who supported him while he was writing this book throughout the pandemic; he could not have done this without their kindness, generosity, and encouragement.

This book was written using similar tools to those described in this text, and it would not have been possible without current advances in technology, including cloud-based computing and collaboration, videoconferencing, and various productivity and graphic design software. We wrote this text across five time zones, three countries, and through many email notifications. We were privileged to access these technologies and know firsthand the impact that they can have on youth, families, and educators alike. The juxtaposition of the COVID-19 pandemic on school teleconsultation created a newfound importance for this work on a global scale.

PART I FOUNDATIONS OF SCHOOL TELECONSULTATION

INTRODUCTION: FOUNDATIONS OF SCHOOL TELECONSULTATION

School teleconsultation refers to a broad array of indirect services that use telecommunications technologies to increase accessibility, efficiency, and equity in consultation service provision. In these indirect services, a consultant collaborates with a consultee or group of consultees (e.g., educators, caregivers, community service providers) to support socially meaningful outcomes for clients or service recipients (e.g., students, school staff; see Figure PI.1). The teleconsultation process is a form of telehealth, in which telecommunications technologies are used to address a variety of medical and behavioral health concerns between the provider and the student. Numerous related professions often participate in the teleconsultation process to address referrals that can be systemic or highly individualized (see Figure PI.2). In the previous few decades, several major technological advancements have shifted the access to this technology, from features available only in major university and hospital research centers to hardware and software that most people can access in their pocket at any time. And this trend is continuing to expand access to services and supports across remote and underserved communities. Every year, new telecommunications technologies are developed, and costs decrease on available options; this is increasing access and affordability.

These services can include a variety of synchronous and asynchronous technologies, such as videoconferencing, text message, email, phone calls, or audio and video recordings. *Synchronous*, or real-time, technologies allow for live interactions between the consultant and the consultee. These can be

FIGURE PI.1. The School Teleconsultation Process

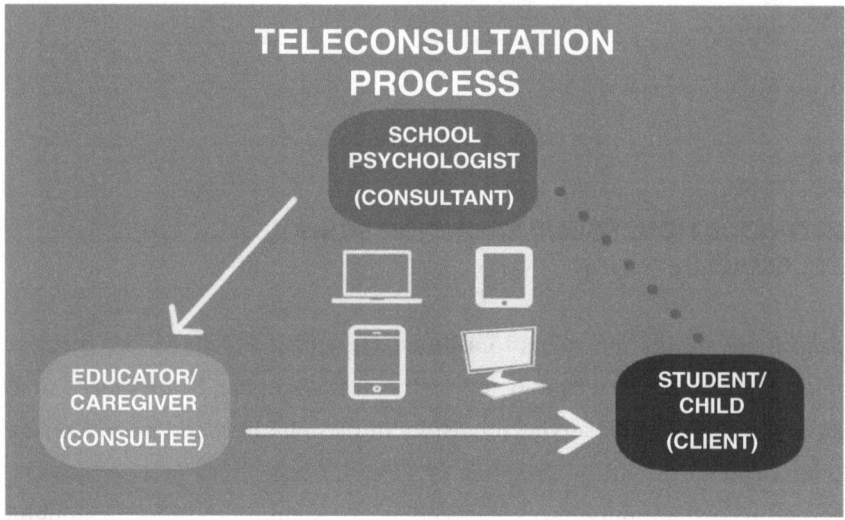

in the form of videoconferencing, phone calls, or text messages to communicate with one another. *Asynchronous* technologies, on the other hand, use a combination of store-and-forward platforms to communicate in a delayed fashion. This format may use written text, audio recordings, or video recordings to send communications between the consultant and consultee across platforms such as email, cloud-based storage platforms, text message, or voicemail. School teleconsultation may be exclusively practiced using virtual or online services, whereas in other cases, some consultants may incorporate a blended or hybrid service delivery model that uses a combination of in-person and online services to address the referral goals. There is no prescriptive set of required technology or types of service provision to qualify as school teleconsultation. Rather, there are many ways, which we review in this book, to practice school teleconsultation.

The purpose of this book is to provide the context and information to support your practice of school teleconsultation. Part I reviews historical, ethical, and contextual factors that influence how school teleconsultation developed into the practice that it is today. This is the key knowledge that

FIGURE PI.2. Levels of Support in School Teleconsultation

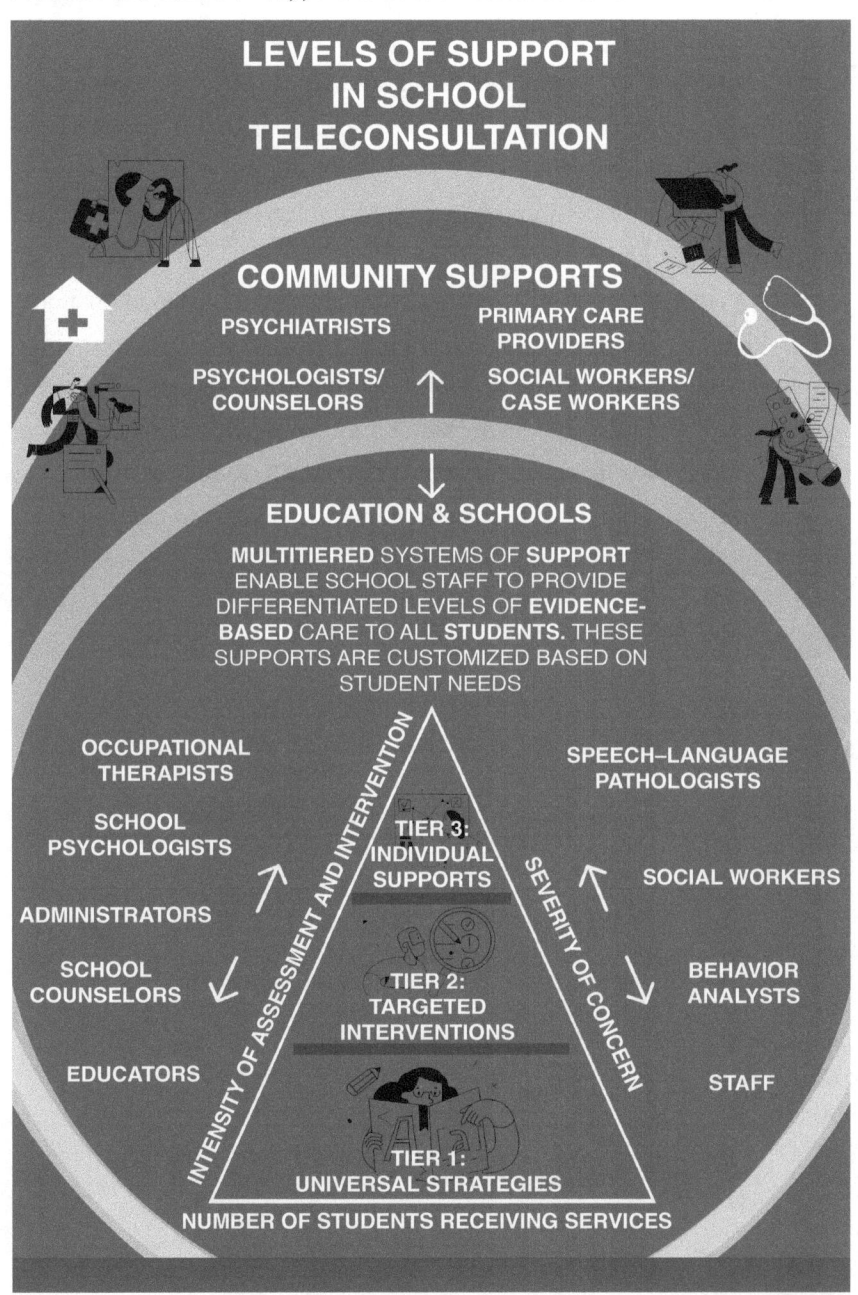

will inform your daily practice. The chapters in Part II function as a practical guide by offering step-by-step instructions, tips to strengthen your practice, and troubleshooting strategies to support the practice of anyone—from a novice to an expert—in school teleconsultation. In Part III, we conclude with a discussion of current barriers to school teleconsultation and where the service modality, teleconsultation, is heading in the future. Where appropriate, we have included discussions of increased equity and access to services through teleconsultation.

To supplement the book, we provide a number of companion materials, which can be found online (https://www.u-tteclab.com/book--text-resources.html). These include graphics that further illustrate the concepts that we describe in the subsequent chapters, as well as illustrated versions of the case studies that appear at the end of Chapters 3 through 7.

As you orient yourself to the content in the text, understanding key terms will be helpful, both conceptually and practically. Table PI.1 lists various key terms related to teleconsultation.

TABLE PI.1. Key Terms

Term	Definition
Telehealth	The process of delivering medical and behavioral health services using telecommunications technologies
Telecommunication technologies	Any platform that facilitates communication to one or more individuals—these include videoconferencing, phone, email, text messaging
School teleconsultation	A broad scope of indirect services using telecommunications technologies to increase accessibility, efficiency, and equity in service provision in educational contexts
Consultant	Individual who provides support, training, and expertise related to socially valid outcomes related to the student and/or educator
Consultee	Individual who receives support from a consultant and ultimately uses those skills to improve outcomes for their student (i.e., client)
Student	Client or individual who directly benefits from the interventions or procedures that the consultee uses to improve relevant outcomes
Synchronous	Real-time technologies that allow for live interactions between the consultant and consultee

TABLE PI.1. Key Terms (*Continued*)

Term	Definition
Asynchronous	All activities that occur through technologies in an engage-when-convenient fashion—this process can occur through videos, email, and files, which are accessible anytime
In-person	Service provision where the participants are in the same physical space
Online	Service provision in which the participants are in different physical spaces and use telecommunications technologies
Face-to-face	The process of engaging with an individual, in real time, where the faces of each person are oriented toward one another—this can be online, through videoconferencing, or in person
Videoconferencing	The process of communicating through real-time audio and video technology
Cloud-based storage	A system for storing, managing, and collaborating data and files through an internet server accessible to individuals with appropriate permissions
Telepresence robots	Hardware that individuals can use to increase engagement and accessibility within a videoconferencing experience by moving or looking around a space—these include mobile and stationary versions
Virtual reality	A fully digital, immersive, simulated environment that allows individuals to interact with avatars or objects approximative to in-person spaces
Augmented reality	A digitally enhanced and immersive environment that allows individuals to interact with avatars or objects approximative to in-person spaces

1 THE HISTORICAL CONTEXT OF SCHOOL TELECONSULTATION

For more than a century, the practice of consultation has been ever shifting and adapting to meet the needs of the time. Some of the earliest psychology services began as a consultative approach wherein psychologists practicing in a clinic setting were providing services to address school problems and the mental health needs of students (Alpert, 1976). Historically, school psychologists have been burdened with psychological assessment in schools and have not had the time to address students' behavioral and mental health needs. Although some school psychologists were providing consultation in their roles, clinical psychologists and psychiatrists have been influential in addressing these needs for students and families.

These early providers used both indirect and direct services to address the mental and behavioral health needs of their students. For example, Lightner Witmer's early work in psychology, from the beginning of the 20th century, included both school-based services and direct services in clinics to address the referred concerns of caregivers, teachers, and school administrators (Fagan, 1996). Through a series of observations, assessments, and interviews with teachers and families, Witmer would conceptualize a case and develop services for that individual student or adult. Many of these early services involved

---

https://doi.org/10.1037/0000366-001
Teleconsultation in Schools: A Guide to Collaborative Practice, by A. J. Fischer and B. S. Bloomfield
Copyright © 2024 by the American Psychological Association. All rights reserved.

consultation with other professionals and collaboration with teachers and caregivers to address the individual referrals. These early efforts took the field of school psychology to a position where consultation and collaboration were an influential part of the provision of related services. The early part of the 20th century emphasized the services provided; however, no formal model of consultation was widely recognized at that time (Warren, 2018).

Consultation services started to grow more significantly following World War II, with the work of Gerald Caplan. Caplan and his small team of providers were responsible for addressing the needs of approximately 16,000 youth who had recently immigrated to Israel (Caplan & Caplan, 1999). With the overwhelming referrals for all of those youth, a more efficient service delivery model was needed to support their mental health needs. In addition to logistical barriers related to such a large caseload, Caplan and his colleagues experienced geographical barriers due to distance and difficulty in providing traditional in-person services. With the significant amount of time to travel between locations, and limited time at each location, the clinicians noted that they were spending more time talking with and collaborating with the adults who worked with the youth daily than directly providing psychotherapy with youth. Thus, the model of *counseling the counselors* was developed (Caplan & Caplan, 1999). By providing support and recommendations to instructors in crisis, the psychologists were able to address the highest need referrals and increase instructor capacity to navigate similar challenges in the future.

This work further developed into the model of *mental health consultation*, where the consultant engages with a consultee to prevent and treat relevant mental health outcomes (Caplan & Caplan, 1999). This can be done in a variety of ways. Predominantly, mental health consultation can be described across four types, depending on the referral and current need: student-centered case consultation, consultee-centered case consultation, program-centered administrative consultation, and consultee-centered administrative consultation. They differ by who is central to the outcome (student, consultee, or system) as well as whether there is a specific referral (i.e., case) or an organizational-wide concern (i.e., administrative). While this model was predominantly developed outside of the school system, this framework aligns with some of the early school psychology work in efforts to increase efficiency and access to mental and behavioral health services.

Consultation, traditionally, has been practiced with an external expert serving the role of the consultant. In this approach, the consultant is not a part of the system in which they are consulting, and they use their previous experience and expertise to shape the behavior of the consultees to indirectly support behavior change in the students. School-based consultation differs in practice, as well, from earlier demonstrations of consultation in that the consultant may be a part of the school system. Here, the school consultant may be a school psychologist or other mental and behavioral health professional employed by the school district to support behavior change of the teachers and students within their schools.

Meyers (1973) proposed an adaptation of mental health consultation for school-based services. Meyers's four-level model of school psychological consultation varied in how indirect the services were between the consultant and student. Level I is *direct service to the child*, where the school consultant provides direct psychoeducational assessment with the student to support intervention planning in the school; this aligns with similar assessment services conducted today, where results may impact student placement. Level II is *indirect service to the child*, where through working with the teacher, the consultant changes environmental variables, which results in changes in observable behavior in the student. Level III is *direct services to the teacher*, where the school psychologist provides psychological services to the teacher to change the teacher's behavior. While changes in student behavior also may be observed, the primary goal is changes in teacher behavior. Finally, Level IV is *service to the school system*. In this level, the targeted behavior change involves groups of individuals at the schoolwide level; this may include a group of teachers, administrators, or support staff. This still results in changes to student behavior; however, student behavior change is a secondary goal.

Concurrently, alternative theoretical models to consultation were being codified in the field of school psychology, including *organizational consultation* and *behavioral consultation* (Lambert, 1974; Reschly, 1976). These various models were rising in popularity as different ways to increase the efficacy and access to school-based services while expanding the school psychologist's role beyond the psychometrician testing and placing children in alternative education settings. Whereas the organizational consultant supports the school system, administration, and groups of teachers, a behavioral consultant follows an operant approach assessing the individualized contextual and environmental variables that immediately precede (i.e., antecedent) and follow (i.e., consequence) the behavior of concern (Bergan & Caldwell, 1967).

The *behavioral consultation* model—or more contemporarily called *problem-solving consultation*—is an approach to consultation that, while applied in various settings, has been a frequent approach to school-based consultation (Kratochwill & Bergan, 1990). Although published 25 years ago, the predominant model of consultation in published studies has historically been a behavioral consultation approach (Sheridan, Welch, & Orme, 1996). In Sheridan, Welch, and Orme's (1996) review of consultation outcomes from 1985 to 1995, 46% of published studies used behavioral consultation or one of its variants, whereas previous reviews of consultation outcomes have found similar patterns. This approach defines the goals for consultation in objective, behavioral terms and uses frequent measurement to assess change in the target behavior. (Note: This is the primary theoretical approach to teleconsultation that we cover throughout the practical guide in this text.) To accomplish this goal, the problem-solving approach has followed four primary stages:

1. problem identification
2. problem analysis
3. treatment implementation
4. treatment evaluation

These four stages are progressed through systematically and sequentially, following measured changes in the observed behavior (Kratochwill & Bergan, 1990). In this traditional approach, the relationship is triadic—as the consultant works with the consultee and they implement changes to impact the student. With the understanding that the relationship between the consultee and consultant is of critical importance to effective problem solving, an additional stage was added: rapport building (Erchul & Martens, 2010). This stage comes first in the problem-solving process, as the consultant needs to develop a working alliance with the consultee to best gather relevant information and collaborate throughout the referral.

A variation of this problem-solving approach adds a fourth party to the assessment and intervention process: a caregiver. In conjoint behavioral consultation, the consultation team includes the consultant, a teacher, a caregiver, and the student. As behavioral and academic challenges are observed not only in the classroom, you should collaborate with the many relevant community partners in a student's life to best support their needs. Where conjoint behavioral consultation excels is by partnering with the student's teacher and caregiver to develop an ecologically appropriate treatment plan and bridge the gap between home and school (Sheridan et al., 2008). Unfortunately, traditional formats of teacher and caregiver training are costly, are time intensive, and require resources that are often limited in many homes and schools (Kratochwill et al., 2003).

EARLY TECHNOLOGY

Since the foundation of the field of school psychology, practice has been shifting and improving to align with the best available evidence to support students. With that, each advancement has strived to match the technological advances of the time. With the rapid adoption of personal computers and related technologies, school psychologists have become more effective, efficient, and accessible than ever before (Florell, 2011). While many of the relevant technologies that we discuss may have been available earlier on, most of the advancements in technology for school psychology practice began to be seen in the 1980s, with many applications moving from novel to ubiquitous in the field over the past 40 years.

In 1984, the journal *School Psychology Review* published a special issue on microcomputers in school psychology. The early uses of technology in the field of school psychology predominantly centered on meeting the needs of the practitioner—many school psychologists used computers to assist with report writing, test scoring, and data management (McCullough & Wenck, 1984). While there were some applications for test administration and telecommunications in use, the majority of school psychologists were using computers to increase efficiency with the same tasks they were completing prior to the use of computers.

Regarding telecommunications, the primary forms of computer use were for "electronic mail," or email, and "electronic bulletin boards," or web forums and discussion boards (McCullough & Wenck, 1984, p. 435). The practitioner could send a message to either a specific person (i.e., email) or post to a group page (i.e., web forum) to answer questions or receive feedback from their peers. Importantly, information found through the telecommunications networks could then be printed for review. Today, there have been many advances in the technology relevant for communication and consultation practices. First, we review some of the history of the various technologies and their early applications to consultation.

Video Observation

A keystone to behavioral consultation involves the direct observation of students and teachers in the classroom. Traditionally, this has been done with the consultant sitting in the back corner of the classroom. With developing video-recording technology, Kent and colleagues (1979) sought to evaluate whether comparable data for behavior observations could be gleaned from a closed-circuit television as from sitting in the classroom and found that there were no significant differences across conditions. This demonstrated that accurate and reliable data collection could be conducted using early technology, including live video observation.

Audio Feedback

In the early examples of videos in schools, feedback was provided asynchronously. The use of live, real-time performance feedback is an important advancement beyond the previously described video observations. Integrating real-time performance feedback through audio transmission, also called *bug-in-the-ear* (BITE), has been demonstrated in schools for more than 70 years (Korner & Brown, 1952). BITE technology uses a headphone or audio receiver for the consultee, while the consultant provides audio feedback through a microphone from a distance. This has been instrumental in teacher, psychometrician, and psychologist training in schools (e.g., Baum & Lane, 1976; Bowles & Nelson, 1976; Scheeler & Lee, 2002). The earliest forms of the technology included a wire connecting an earpiece and a chest microphone to an observation room behind a one-way mirror (Korner & Brown, 1952). Korner and Brown (1952) called the device "the mechanical third ear." Recent examples of BITE include radio, mobile phones, wireless internet, and Bluetooth technology (e.g., Scheeler & Lee, 2002). Technology has progressed greatly since the mechanical third ear, yet the premise of the technology tool remains the same: to increase the efficacy of performance feedback. With increased use and availability of videoconferencing technology, many researchers and practitioners have combined BITE with videoconferencing to conduct live staff coaching remotely (Rosenberg & Huntington, 2021).

Video Modeling

Beginning in the early 1980s, Webster-Stratton and colleagues (1988) evaluated the use of videotaped parent training to address behavioral concerns in the home. The team developed a 10- to 12-session video-modeling program to demonstrate skills useful for the caregiver in the home. Parents watched these videos on a television screen in a clinic, and each session comprised a series of vignettes in which the parent was observed implementing a behavioral strategy with their child, while receiving performance feedback. After watching these video vignettes in individual or group formats, parents demonstrated a significant increase in skills, and, concurrently, there was an observed reduction in problem behavior in their home (Webster-Stratton et al., 1988).

Following some of that earlier work, Kratochwill and colleagues (2003) sought to identify a more efficient training process for conjoint behavioral consultation. To address some of the challenges about high costs, they then evaluated two training programs—a written manual and a videotape series—to teach new skills to address student behavioral difficulties. Parents and teachers received either a written manual to address behaviors of concern, or the written manual and a set of videotapes, as developed by Webster-Stratton (1981). When compared with the direct parent training via video-modeling literature, this application of video modeling within a consultation format was less robust; however, methodological concerns (including small sample sizes and high attrition) need to be considered (Kratochwill et al., 2003). Parents and teachers found the intervention to be highly acceptable, and most reported high levels of treatment integrity following video modeling.

Distance Education

Distance education is the provision of training and educational services across great distances using synchronous and asynchronous technologies, such as videoconferencing, recorded lectures, readings, discussion forums, and learning management software platforms. While many of these technologies are embedded in current training courses (both in-person and online education; Fischer et al., 2020), many of these technological contributions to training have been influential in the more modern practice of school teleconsultation.

Synchronous online training requires a stable internet connection and sufficient bandwidth to support two-way audio and video transmissions. The first forms of distance education used computers with telephone or satellite connections to connect across great distances (Howard et al., 1992). When internet access was more limited, providers would need to sacrifice some of the more advanced features, including two-way video. The learner would connect their computer to a modem to access written or graphic information on the internet and then call in to the training course through a second telephone line to have audio support this graphic medium. Dial-up internet would require two lines (one for computer communication and a second for telephone audio transmission; Howard et al., 1992). Satellite communications, on the other hand, could increase access to some learners; however, a phone line was still needed for synchronous audio transmission, and it could be quite costly. Using a satellite connection, the learner could receive an audio/video feed of the instructor and then use a phone line to support two-way audio. At that time in the early 1990s, two-way video was not feasible using dial-up internet or satellite connections (Howard et al., 1992). Fiber-optic connections, however, did allow for two-way video feeds, including videoconferencing.

Throughout the 1990s, there were significant increases in computer capability—and with concurrent reductions in costs, access to computer technologies increased rapidly. However, some distance education programs in psychology and education were still falling behind these trends (Belar, 1998). Belar (1998) proposed the use of CD-ROMs for self-paced computer training of future psychologists: The student would review the materials on the disc on their personal computer, independently complete all learning of the core knowledge components, and then use in-person sessions with the faculty to rehearse skills and receive more performance feedback. While accessible and advantageously utilizing the technology of the time, CD-ROM training would still require mailing or exchanging the discs in person to facilitate this training program.

The conversation about integrating technology into practice continued into the 21st century. A major theme of the 2002 multisite conference on the Future of School Psychology was the use of technology as a tool for dissemination and communication (Dawson et al., 2004). Technological applications in distance education for school psychologists were still in their infancy, and greater development was still needed to catch up to the technological advancements of the time. Now, some 20 years later, online education, personal computing, and internet services have progressed to a point that many individuals access the internet daily and most training courses involve some form of online learning (Fischer et al., 2020).

Videoconferencing

Videoconferencing combines the technologies of audio and video transmission to support video observation, audio feedback, and video modeling synchronously and over great distances. The previous literature predominantly demonstrated these advancements in-person, where the consultant would still be required to be in the school to record or transmit the audio/video. While there were several benefits for incorporating that technology, the previous advancements did not address the barriers of distance, travel time, and costs related to service delivery.

Telecommunications training formats in schools have been in practice for decades (Stowitschek et al., 1986). These early forms of using multiple modalities to provide training and support to teachers were effective at addressing the barrier of distance; however, the training content and process were similar to traditionally conducted-in-person in-service training. Stowitschek et al. (1986) stated that at this time, "the interactive potential of telecommunications has hardly been tapped" (p. 28). To best use this technology to improve services, they recommended, the teleconsultant should work directly with the teacher in the classroom, in situ, rather than restricting telecommunications meetings to separate training sessions outside of the classroom. This allows the teleconsultant to directly conduct video observations, provide in-the-moment feedback (e.g., BITE), and model desired behavior for the teacher.

The technology has progressed a long way from two-way audio/video communications in the 1980s. Early demonstrations of videoconferencing used a microwave connection paired with a laser link to connect teleconsultants with a classroom approximately 275 miles away (Stowitschek et al., 1986). This was possible due only to a university partnership that had an established telecommunications network. While the technology was not feasible for everyday use at that time, teachers were able to learn new skills in behavior management and classroom instruction over videoconferencing. Further, this technology was feasible for live observations in the classroom with performance feedback. By using videoconferencing, the teleconsultant saved time and increased their access to school partners, and the schools saved significant money in additional costs associated with in-person services.

Unfortunately, 20 years later, there were still limited demonstrations of videoconferencing in school practice. Clopton and Knesting (2006) found that travel time remained a significant barrier for rural school psychologists, as it impacted the latter's service provision. Thus, Clopton and Knesting recommended that videoconferencing be explored further for addressing school needs in consultation, supervision, and collaborative meetings. More recently, we have started to see greater demonstrations of the use of videoconferencing to support schools across greater distances (e.g., H. C. King et al., 2021). Many of the future demonstrations of school-based videoconferencing are described in greater detail in the following section.

SCHOOL TELECONSULTATION

Although technology has been applied in a variety of ways to school consultation practice, applications of a model of school teleconsultation have been limited until recently. Many of the early applications came from the field of behavior analysis, where behavior analysts were providing consultation to local providers in schools. For example, behavior analysts affiliated with the Biobehavioral Service clinic at the University of Iowa collaborated via teleconsultation with local providers in rural schools 145 to 193 kilometers from their clinic in order to conduct brief functional analyses in the schools (Barretto et al., 2006). In one case, Barretto and colleagues (2006) used a phone interview, prior to the functional analysis, to develop hypotheses, whereas in the other case, the researchers used a mailed questionnaire and descriptive observation conducted in person by a local provider. Then, they used videoconferencing to conduct the functional analyses. The teleconsultants observed each session, visually inspected the data, and provided feedback throughout. The functional analyses were conducted by local providers with high fidelity, allowing the teleconsultants to provide high-quality support.

In a systematic review of school teleconsultation, H. C. King et al. (2021) identified 13 studies that included triadic school-based services with K–12 students. All studies included were published in 2009 or later, with the majority of studies reporting individual student-level data. According to H. C. King and colleagues (2021), one of the earlier examples of school teleconsultation was conducted by Machalicek et al. (2009), who trained teachers to conduct preference assessments with students on the autism spectrum using videoconferencing technologies. *Preference assessments* (Hagopian et al., 2004) are systematic procedures that educators, caregivers, and therapists can use to identify potential desired circumstances, items, or individuals in the environment. Through preference assessments, providers can use identified stimuli to encourage behavior change. The consultant in the Machalicek et al. study used a computer with a webcam to observe and provide vocal feedback to the teacher on their implementation fidelity in the classroom. The teacher used a laptop computer with a webcam and a Bluetooth headset to communicate with the consultant during implementation of the preference assessment. During the observation sessions, all teachers implemented the protocol with 100% fidelity (Machalicek et al., 2009). Following the preference assessment, the consultant designed an individualized intervention based on the results of the preference assessment and trained the teachers to implement the intervention in their classroom.

Many of the early examples of teleconsultation used it for behavior assessment, including functional analyses. Using both synchronous and asynchronous technologies, Frieder and colleagues (2009) trained a teacher and a speech–language pathologist to conduct a functional analysis in their classroom. The approach blended in-person and online meetings throughout the teleconsultation process: Rapport building and initial training were conducted in person, while further interactions were online using web-based technologies. The functional analysis was able to be observed through videoconferencing; however, the researchers used a video recording for data collection, as the internet connection limited live data analysis due to restrictions on internet speed at the school.

Teleconsultation has also been applied in the design, training, and ongoing measurement of a classroom-based intervention for a child with autism (Gibson et al., 2010). Like some of the other early examples, Gibson and colleagues (2010) used teleconsultation to address limitations that were impacting their ability to provide services. While the initial functional behavior assessment was conducted in person, teleconsultation was used for ongoing consultation in order to address barriers of distance between the consultant and the school in which they were providing services. A combination of emailed written instruction and videoconferencing for modeling, rehearsal, and performance feedback was used to train staff in the use of functional communication training to reduce the frequency of elopement in the classroom. However, there were still limitations related to Internet speed and hardware capabilities that inhibited teleconsultation applications.

Challenges reported with teleconsultation include the teleconsultant's inability to see all angles of the observation room, the audio/video feed cuts out, and the video quality inhibits accurate data collection. As the capabilities of internet connectivity, hardware technology, and software continue to expand, the applications of teleconsultation also have been expanding to take advantage of those features. With the proliferation of high-speed internet connectivity and more advanced processors, most commercially available telecommunications products can maintain a two-way videoconference for teleconsultation.

Similarly, these advancements can be used with other novel technologies. For example, telepresence robots have been used to increase the field of view, move around the school, and increase accessibility of videoconferencing participation (Bloomfield et al., 2020; Fischer, Bloomfield, et al., 2019; Fischer, Clark, et al., 2019). Fischer, Bloomfield, et al. (2019) used telepresence robots as a part of a comprehensive teleconsultation model in a rural school. The consultant would remotely sign on and drive the robot within the school to observe the students in the target classroom, requiring limited setup from the consultee school. This was an effective modality for conducting teleconsultation, and the teachers found it acceptable. Bloomfield et al. (2020) used telepresence robots while conducting functional analyses in rural schools. In addition to supporting greater visibility of the students' behavior, the telepresence robot was used with BITE technology to observe and provide feedback on the consultee's implementation fidelity. The remote control of the telepresence robots allowed the teleconsultant to make in-the-moment adjustments to the camera in order to maintain the optimal viewing angle.

While all of these examples have focused predominantly on the teleconsultant, teacher, and individual student, teleconsultation also has applications for schoolwide supports (McDaniel et al., 2020; McDaniel & Bloomfield, 2020). McDaniel and Bloomfield (2020) used videoconferencing to support a rural school district with their implementation of School-Wide Positive Behavioral Interventions and Supports (SW-PBIS). Using already-existing technology, the teleconsultant would join the SW-PBIS team meetings to provide coaching on their assessment and implementation practices. Following 1 year conducting teleconsultation, the schools demonstrated adequate fidelity of schoolwide practices, and team meetings were conducted with high fidelity. While that preliminary evidence supports teleconsultation for schoolwide practices, information gathered about the teleconsultation recipients' experiences was limited.

ACCEPTABILITY AND PRACTICALITY OF TELECONSULTATION

Much of the literature on school teleconsultation has consisted of brief case studies and single-case research design. In a departure from this, Fischer and colleagues (2016) compared in-person and videoconferencing services for completing the problem identification interview across 60 classroom teachers. The classroom teachers participated in a simulated in-person and video-conference interview with a consultant and rated their perceived acceptability both before and after. Fischer et al. (2016) found that teachers with no previous exposure to teleconsultation found the procedure acceptable for discussing a student referral, and there was an increase in acceptability after exposure to a synthesized teleconsultation meeting.

While evidence supports positive student outcomes, and consultees generally find the procedure acceptable, there are ways in which the process itself may differ. Fischer et al. (2017) sought to address that by using the consultation analysis record to investigate content and process variables within teleconsultation meetings. They analyzed the verbal behavior of consultants during both in-person and videoconference consultation sessions in order to determine whether there were different patterns of utterances across the two different media. They found that consultants tended to say fewer statements over videoconferencing than in person; however, videoconference sessions had more content relevance, process effectiveness, and interview control. Teleconsultants' verbal behavior tended to be more on-topic and succinct than in-person comparisons (Fischer et al., 2017); when meetings are in-person, conversations naturally drift and flow between topics, and nonverbal cues add additional information. Some of this context is missed during video-conferencing, and that was hypothesized as being part of the difference in ratings between in-person and videoconference sessions. These patterns of verbal behavior are aligned with effective teleconsultation outcomes, indicating that the process of teleconsultation can also be effective to address referral concerns.

In a follow-up to McDaniel and Bloomfield (2020), McDaniel and colleagues (2020) conducted a series of focus groups with rural school team members who had participated in teleconsultation to receive remote coaching. Overall, the focus group participants found teleconsultation to be an effective and efficient way to receive support in SW-PBIS implementation.

Teleconsultation is designed to help address barriers to effective service—this includes addressing affordability, practicality, and access. This has been highlighted previously for providers in remote and underserved communities (e.g., Bloomfield et al., 2020; Fischer, Bloomfield, et al., 2019; McDaniel & Bloomfield, 2020). Schultz et al. (2018) surveyed school psychologists about those psychologists' beliefs regarding teleconsultation, in order to analyze the variables that influence the school psychologists' decisions to adopt teleconsultation to address behavioral referrals. When the commute was longer than 30 minutes, most school psychologists reported that they would be interested in teleconsultation, yet that likelihood decreased with a corresponding decrease in the teleconsultant's familiarity with the technology. School psychologists tended to be more likely to prefer in-person consultation when they had less familiarity with technology or when the student referral was more "serious" or "unusual" (Schultz et al., 2018). While contexts might still indicate times when in-person consultation is warranted, there is increasing evidence that teleconsultation is a feasible and acceptable modality to support students in schools.

CONCLUSION

Teleconsultation is a means to create equity and access to effective interventions. For decades, technological advancements have been increasing the affordability of required hardware, and generational differences support that the ever-growing majority will be familiar with the use of teleconsultation. As additional technological advances proliferate school practice, more students will be able to access evidence-based services through teleconsultation, irrespective of location. This chapter reviewed the history of school teleconsultation in relation to the developments in technology over the past century. While there has been great progress recently, there is still more work to be done. We explore future research directions and applications for teleconsultation in Chapter 9.

2 PROFESSIONAL AND ETHICAL ISSUES IN SCHOOL TELECONSULTATION

There are several laws and ethical guidelines that guide our practice. In the United States, school psychologists are governed by the National Association of School Psychologists (NASP; 2020a) and their *Principles for Professional Ethics*. Practitioners may also be guided by the ethical standards of the American Psychological Association's (APA's; 2017) *Ethical Principles of Psychologists and Code of Conduct* (APA Ethics Code) for psychologists and the Behavior Analyst Certification Board (BACB; 2020) for behavior analysts. In many cases, the ethical standards of the profession might be more stringent than local law; however, it is important that practitioners follow local law and uphold the ethical standards to best support the students, staff, and families with whom they work.

Many of the standards align with ethical teleconsultation practices; however, more recent publications specifically address the impact of technology and social media in practice. For example, NASP (2020a) specifies social media and technology within the index of ethical principles. They highlight the most relevant standards to an evolving technological landscape. In a different stance, BACB (2020) stipulates a subsection of their guidance on public statements to specify how social media can and cannot be used in

---

https://doi.org/10.1037/0000366-002
Teleconsultation in Schools: A Guide to Collaborative Practice, by A. J. Fischer and B. S. Bloomfield
Copyright © 2024 by the American Psychological Association. All rights reserved.

public statements representing the profession. APA (2017), however, has less specific language in their ethical principles related to technology. It is noteworthy that both NASP and BACB recently published updates to their ethical standards, whereas APA currently uses the 2002 APA Ethics Code with minor amendments in 2010 and 2016.

The following sections identify specific ethical issues relevant to the practice of teleconsultation under the four major themes outlined in the NASP *Principles for Professional Ethics*. While references to some other professional ethical standards are made throughout, our discussion is organized in this manner.

RESPECTING THE DIGNITY OF ALL PERSONS

Teleconsultants often work with multiple parties while providing services. These frequently include students, educators, school administrators, and families. Thus, efforts should be made to respect the dignity of all of these individuals during service delivery, while centering the student experience in all decisions. This begins prior to initiating services through the consent and assent process. Informed consent is required when the consultation is likely to be ongoing, extensive, and intrusive to an individual's privacy (Guiding Principle I.1; NASP, 2020a). This is particularly relevant for external teleconsultants who are not employed by the school district. In those cases, consent is required prior to initiating services. The consent process during teleconsultation must

- be clearly described,
- be written to be understood by the relevant parties,
- communicate all aspects of service delivery, and
- specify how the participant's information will be protected.

This consent process can be completed using a paper form—or, in some cases, a digital signature is acceptable. A teleconsultant may need to have the form printed, signed on paper, and then returned to them for their records. Unique to teleconsultation, the consent process should review details of the technology used, efforts to maintain privacy, and security features of the platform. When possible, and indicated, you should seek assent from the student(s) as well, so that all parties are properly informed of the intervention process and each can participate as active members of the team.

Teleconsultants should respect the right of people to decide whether to disclose private information and must maintain confidentiality within the boundaries of the laws in which they practice (Guiding Principle I.2; NASP, 2020a). In many cases, school providers may use an employer-provided email address and device (e.g., laptop, mobile phone) to communicate with teachers and families. Email is not a private form of communication; information shared by email and stored on school district servers may be accessed by the employer (Demers & Sullivan, 2016). Thus, emails may be a part of the teleconsultant's employment record or the student's educational file.

Prior to initiating services, and in subsequent meetings, you should review the boundaries of confidentiality. As some meetings may be from a person's home or other casual setting, the consultee or student may be more comfortable disclosing personal information, and other personal information may be gleaned inadvertently from the visible surroundings. Frequently restating the boundaries of confidentiality will help prompt participants to be aware of sensitive disclosures. To help protect their privacy, you can instruct the other parties about using a filter or virtual background on videoconference meetings. This will restrict your ability to view the surroundings in the participant's private environment. Similarly, headphones will help protect the student's and consultee's privacy by restricting the amplification of audio signals for others to hear in the environment.

You should intentionally promote fairness, equity, and justice in all of your work. As a teleconsultant, you are working with a school to support improved practices. Through this effort, you may observe or learn about discriminatory or unfair practices. You should not engage in these practices and must make every effort feasible to correct for these actions (Guiding Principle I.3; NASP, 2020a). On the contrary, through teleconsultation, you may be able to increase outreach, so that all individuals can access needed support through technology or resources.

PROFESSIONAL COMPETENCE AND RESPONSIBILITY

In any practice within allied health, practitioners are bound to provide only services within their scope of competence; this is true also within teleconsultation (Guiding Principle II.1; NASP, 2020a). Competence within teleconsultation relates to the practice of teleconsultation itself as well as professional competence in the referral domain in which the teleconsultant is practicing. Developing competencies in the specific referrals is outside the scope of this book. Reading relevant materials, such as this text, is one component of developing competencies in teleconsultation. Further, you should seek out supervision and professional development from teleconsultants with expertise in this service delivery model.

You can develop these competencies in teleconsultation, as well, using a behavioral skills training approach. In behavioral skills training, the practitioner receives didactic training on teleconsultation service by attending a presentation or reading a guide on the topic, then the practitioner observes a model (prerecorded video or live model) of an individual successfully engaging in that skill, followed by rehearsal in the presence of an expert on teleconsultation service delivery. The expert trainer provides feedback to the practitioner until the practitioner demonstrates competency.

It is your responsibility to assess the appropriateness of the referral for teleconsultation services and to ensure that the referral is within your scope of practice. When the service needs are beyond your scope, refer to other service providers. Alternatively, if the service requires additional support or is complex in presentation, consider transitioning to in-person services. In cases where remote support is insufficient and the consultee requires more direct modeling and intervention, teleconsultation services may be inappropriate. Such circumstance would require a different level of involvement from the consultant.

Technology is useful in supporting documentation and monitoring progress. This is a critical area of ethical and professional practice for teleconsultants, who should verify and report relevant data regarding the cases in which they consult. Simply, you can use a word processor or spreadsheet as a communication log to keep track of all relevant communication with the school and family. This log is useful in verifying the frequency and scope of all contact between parties. Emails can also be retained as a permanent product of digital communication; they can be saved to a folder in the consultant's inbox or exported as a PDF and stored in a relevant storage folder. You can use a variety of permanent products, such as recorded videos and work samples, to collect data and analyze asynchronously. Automation can be used for accurate data collection, with advances in computer algorithms and commercially available sensors that streamline the process. For example, to measure the level of noise in a room, the decibel level can be recorded using freely available mobile applications (Radley et al., 2016). Depending on the relevant outcome measured, there are other sensors and platforms that can use technology to facilitate progress monitoring. The data must then all be stored in a secure electronic record. All electronic records must be stored on an encrypted device with password protection to reduce the risk of unexpected exposure of protected information (Guiding Principle II.4; NASP, 2020a). Other national and local laws may also govern the storage of protected health information; consult a local governing body regarding other security requirements for the storage of student information.

Teleconsultation practices allow participants to collaborate from any location, which means that it is easier than ever to include families and students in planning meetings (Fischer & Bloomfield, 2020). Additional family and support personnel can participate while living in distant locations.

Grandparents and other extended family members who may reside outside the student's home can also become active contributors to the assessment and intervention planning. Similarly, teleconsultation easily facilitates involvement of interpreters and other service providers who can communicate in the family's primary language. This is particularly beneficial when there are limited interpreters locally who are competent in a specific language; a qualified interpreter can sign in to a video call from anywhere in the world in order to communicate directly with the family during meetings.

HONESTY AND INTEGRITY IN PROFESSIONAL RELATIONSHIPS

Throughout the teleconsultation process, the consultant must best represent themselves and the profession in which they practice. Ways in which the teleconsultant can virtually represent their qualifications and competencies include

- clarifying credentials in email signatures,
- describing training and expertise on a website about the services delivered,
- accurately noting the limits of any credentials and licenses during initial meetings with consultees, and
- specifying scope of services on any marketing materials.

These ways ethically represent the level of training that each provider may have and clarify the area in which the provider is appropriate to practice. For example, the practice of psychology services in the United States is regulated at the state level, and providers are under different obligations for the states in which they practice (e.g., the state in which the student resides).

Teleconsultants are respectful of other professionals who are working with a student. As the services are conducted remotely, it is easy for other related professionals to virtually join team meetings to support interdisciplinary collaborations. The other professionals can participate in group discussions with the consultee and students, as well as provide consultations to you, as appropriate. You should also limit any multiple relationships when collaborating with students and consultees.

Technology sometimes blurs the line between personal and professional conduct, yet in the field, practitioners often use their platform for professional presentations and communication. You should distinguish clearly between personal and professional social media accounts for any promotion and practice of teleconsultation. The BACB (2020) stipulates, in Section 5.10 of their ethical code, that practitioners should clearly separate personal and professional posting; with any professional social media, explicit consent is needed before you post any information or representation of students. Information about students should not be posted on personal social media channels. Similarly, teleconsultants must obtain informed consent prior to using information about students and consultees during other presentations and provide only statements that are true and aligned with the ethical code (APA, 2017; BACB, 2020; NASP, 2020a).

RESPONSIBILITY TO SCHOOLS, FAMILIES, COMMUNITIES, THE PROFESSION, AND SOCIETY

While some of the work that teleconsultants engage in will be at the individual student or teacher level, you are working within a system with many interacting elements. You also can work at the school or system level in order to promote healthy environments. You can use group-level information to collaborate with school leadership to enact change to support all members of the community.

You are enacting this change, typically, from a distance. That means that the data collected are a small subset of the interactions within the systems. Workplace systems are complex and involve dynamics that are difficult to assess remotely. You must respect and engage in workplace systems in order to enact contextually appropriate and sustainable change. You may not always be able to understand some of the nuances present when interacting only from a distance, and thus you must rely on the local community to provide critical information. Apart from verbal reports, you will observe other behavior, such as body language and responses to recommendations, to assess for the acceptability of teleconsultation services.

Teleconsultation involves a specialized set of skills that can be developed with appropriate training and supervision. Competent teleconsultants are encouraged to train and mentor future teleconsultants. This can be either other currently practicing professionals or graduate students undertaking their training in the field (Guiding Principle IV.4; NASP, 2020a). High-quality, evidence-based training regarding the practice of teleconsultation can be conducted in person or virtually.

COMMON ETHICAL CHALLENGES IN SCHOOL TELECONSULTATION

Published research, best-practice guidelines, and the ethical policy of human service fields must keep up with the rapid development of technology, which leads to professional, legal, and ethical dilemmas with regard to teleconsultation practice. Internet use for professional communication, data analysis, data storage, assessment, and intervention services highlight practices necessary to protect your student's confidentiality and privacy (Demers & Sullivan, 2016). For example, the Health Insurance Portability and Accountability Act of 1996 (HIPAA) is the U.S. federal policy governing the storage and transmission of student information. All student information must remain secure and protected when stored and transmitted digitally; this includes the use of specified platforms, encryption standards, passwords, and related actions on the part of the staff member to ensure all health information remains private. To use the platform, users must comply with these standards and sign a business associate agreement (BAA) in relation to the protection of health information. There are many commercially available health communication and storage platforms that providers can consider that are HIPAA compliant and have signed a BAA.

During the COVID-19 pandemic, however, the Office for Civil Rights (2021) at the U.S. Department of Health and Human Services (HHS) issued a statement offering discretion with enforcement of the HIPAA rules considering good faith efforts to safely provide telehealth services. As the start of the pandemic resulted in a rapid transition to telehealth service provision, HHS noted that providers can use platforms other than the preapproved HIPAA-compliant platforms that maintain private communication between the student and provider. Efforts must be made to protect student information and not use publicly facing platforms (e.g., TikTok, Facebook Live) in order to not be penalized for noncompliance with HIPAA regulations. Today, there is increased clarity from the various telecommunications providers regarding the security of their platform to best protect students; however, it is the practitioner's responsibility to keep up to date with current privacy laws and platform compliance with security standards.

DECISION MAKING IN SCHOOL TELECONSULTATION

Throughout this chapter, we have discussed various ethical and professional issues that may arise during the process of teleconsultation. Because challenges might interfere with the provision of teleconsultation services, the competent teleconsultant must assess the appropriateness of remote service delivery before initiating school teleconsultation. Then, that assessment should be ongoing as contexts can change. The necessity of doing ongoing assessment of the appropriateness of remote service delivery was highlighted at the start of the COVID-19 pandemic, when, due to public health orders, many in-person interactions were deemed a health risk. Cox and colleagues (2020) proposed a decision-making process for risk mitigation for in-person services during the pandemic shutdown period. While the process was recommended primarily for applied behavior analysis (ABA) providers, the recommendations are consistent with other disciplines in teleconsultation: Decisions should be made on a case-by-case basis.

During the 2020–2021 public health crisis, some in-person services needed to be delayed in order to protect the health and safety of the students and service providers (Cox et al., 2020). However, in other cases, the delay in services might cause greater harm. In those instances, alternatives such as teleconsultation should be considered. When teleconsultation is not appropriate, in-person services may be conducted with additional health precautions.

TELECONSULTATION ACCESS

In the home, access to personal computing technology is at an all-time high. A recent Pew Research Center (Perrin, 2021) technology survey indicated that approximately 85% of Americans owned a smartphone, and for those aged 18 to 49, that rate jumped to greater than 96%. Similarly, nearly all public schools in the United States had internet and computer access for students and staff. Furthermore, the survey indicated that three out of every four Americans owned a laptop or desktop computer, while greater than 50% owned a tablet. Thus, for a large percentage of families in the United States, it is reasonable to expect access to devices in the home. Internationally, there is a comparable growth in ownership of similar technology. For example, in most developed countries, the median smartphone ownership in 2019 was 74%; however, this rate was significantly lower in developing countries (e.g., 45%; Silver, 2019). Although the use of student-owned hardware might meet the needs of many teleconsultants, this still leaves millions of individuals without a smartphone, tablet, or computer in the home—especially in low-income and rural communities (Perrin, 2021). Despite the variety of low-cost hardware options, their purchase still requires a financial investment that may be difficult for some schools or families.

For teleconsultation services, the local school or service location should have the facilities and staff to safely conduct the assessment and intervention services. Additionally, all relevant parties should have the requisite technology for services, including reliable internet access. If the consultee or student does not have the requisite technology, you should work to obtain the necessary equipment prior to initiating services. One of your roles is to advocate for equitable access to technology so that all students and staff can participate in learning through using this technology (NASP, 2020b).

After ensuring equitable access to technology, you can engage in problem solving regarding the best procedures to provide telehealth services. Referrals in which there are risks to health and safety may better be served with in-person services or referral to a community provider. School psychologists previously reported that they were less likely to recommend teleconsultation for severe or complex referrals (Schultz et al., 2018). For case referrals within your scope of practice, they are more likely to consider teleconsultation; this is particularly true with greater travel distance between schools.

Providing high-quality care that best meets the needs of the community in which you serve entails many considerations. Teleconsultants navigate ethical, legal, and professional issues throughout their daily practice. It is through intentionality and preemptive planning that they will ensure that all community members have access to evidence-based practices that will support positive outcomes at home and school. Teleconsultation is not the best solution in every circumstance; however, by collaborating and using careful decision making, teleconsultants can embed effective strategies into their work in order to meet the learning and behavioral goals for their consultees and clients.

PART II A PRACTICAL GUIDE TO SCHOOL TELECONSULTATION

INTRODUCTION: A PRACTICAL GUIDE TO SCHOOL TELECONSULTATION

The following chapters provide a practical guide for practitioners, researchers, and trainers to use to inform teleconsultation practice, particularly through a problem-solving consultation framework. This book briefly discusses connections with traditional problem-solving consultation; however, for a comprehensive understanding of the problem-solving consultation procedures, readers should reference the extensive work in this area by influential scholars such as Thomas Kratochwill, Susan Sheridan, William Erchul, Andy Garbacz, and many others. Their work has guided our teleconsultation research, training, and practice, and we highlight the integration of technology within the problem-solving consultation framework.

In this section of the book, we discuss the stages associated with a problem-solving teleconsultation framework, as well as practical considerations that teleconsultants can use and understand for practice in this capacity. The problem-solving teleconsultation framework includes rapport building (Chapter 3), problem identification (Chapter 4), problem analysis (Chapter 5), intervention plan training and implementation (Chapter 6), and intervention plan evaluation (Chapter 7). We have included a teleconsultation infographic in the online resources that shows an overview of this five-step problem-solving teleconsultation framework, and teleconsultants can use this as a quick reference for the process overall or as a tool, in their practice, to share with partners who are curious about the steps and expectations during the teleconsultation process. Similarly, Table PII.1 provides a summary of the goals for each stage of the problem-solving teleconsultation

TABLE PII.1. Problem-Solving Teleconsultation Overview

Stage	Main goals	Data collection	Individual(s) responsible
Stage 1: Rapport building	• Relationship building • Overview of teleconsultation process • Promote inclusiveness and equitable support in teleconsultation • Consent and assent	• Treatment motivation and participation inventories (Parent Motivation Inventory, Barriers to Treatment Participation)	• Teleconsultant
Stage 2: Problem identification	• Identify students' individual characteristics and circumstances • Identify target problem behavior, its antecedents, and its consequences • Establish a plan for data collection and progress monitoring	• Problem identification interview form • Functional behavior assessment • Percentage of on-task behavior • Frequency and intensity of target behavior • Antecedent-behavior-consequence data on target behavior	• Teleconsultant • Consultee • Educator/caregiver
Stage 3: Problem analysis	• Collect antecedent-behavior-consequence data to understand relevant antecedents and consequences of target behavior • Review data collected to inform the problem analysis interview • Assess whether the data collected align with the referral description • Review the frequency of the behavior • Discuss behavior function • Jointly develop a behavior intervention plan and assign roles for implementation	• Problem analysis interview • Indirect and direct assessment measures (e.g., direct observation, semistructured interviews, questionnaires) • Office referrals, grades, and attendance data	• Teleconsultant

Stage	Activities	Measures/Tools	Participants
Stage 4: Plan training and implementation	• Prepare a feasible, ecologically valid, evidence-based intervention and training plan in collaboration with educator • Support ongoing implementation of interventions • Develop a crisis plan and response protocol • Use a systematic training methodology for educators to ensure their acquisition and mastery skills • Provide performance feedback and measurement of implementation fidelity • Monitor progress through daily data collection methods	• Frequency of target problem behavior (consultant) • Reports of academic engagement (teacher) • Behavior intervention plan • Treatment integrity data sheet • Treatment motivation and participation inventories	• Teleconsultant Consultee

Stage 5: Plan evaluation	• Collate data and discuss trends and changes in patterns of behavior using a variety of visual guides
	• Evaluate social validity of the process and outcomes
	• Guide the team through understanding if the teleconsultation goals have been met
	  – If met, plan for the discontinuation of services
	  – If not, identify relevant future modifications
	• Complete acceptability questionnaires
	• After the plan evaluation session, send an email to the consultee and follow up, documenting action items, outline next steps determined in plan evaluation session
		• Plan evaluation interview form
		• Plan evaluation interview objectives checklist
		• Analyze intervention data
		• Intervention Rating Profile
		• Technology Acceptance Model-Fast Form
		• Consultant Evaluation Form
		• Stress/well-being
		• Behavior Intervention Rating Scale
			• Teleconsultant

framework as well as examples of data collection tools and responsible parties at each stage. Further information about each stage is found in the subsequent chapters.

We also present two (fictitious) case studies highlighting the multitiered applications of teleconsultation. In the first case study, we describe a schoolwide teleconsultation experience between a general education classroom teacher and a teleconsultant, with the intention of supporting universal classroom management strategies to improve classwide academic engagement. In the second case study, we describe an intensive teleconsultation collaboration between a special education teacher and a teleconsultant, focusing on an individualized student behavior concern. These case studies provide context at each stage of the problem-solving teleconsultation framework and offer an example of how school teleconsultants might approach their practice. In the subsequent chapters, we revisit the case studies as we proceed through the stages of the problem-solving teleconsultation framework.

CASE STUDY INTRODUCTIONS

Schoolwide Teleconsultation Referral

Zoe (she/her) is a fifth-grade teacher at Mountain Creek Elementary School. She is a White cisgender woman in her mid-20s with an upper middle-class upbringing. Although this is her third year teaching, it is her first time teaching the fifth grade. The previous 2 years, she taught a second-grade class, and the transition has been difficult for her. She finds that the students are acting out more this year than when she was a second-grade teacher, and she is finding it difficult to finish all of her lessons. Students are getting out of their seats, calling out, talking to their friends, and playing on their phones during lessons. Zoe reports that she must frequently stop the lessons in order to redirect the class and address behaviors of concern.

Zoe has previously tried taking away recess and calling home, but it seems as though that hasn't made a difference. She now frequently sends students down to the main office to meet with the school principal, who noticed that Zoe has been sending the same few students there multiple times a week. The principal came and watched a math lesson in Zoe's classroom and observed that while the content of the lesson was of high quality, Zoe was having a difficult time getting her class's attention in order to progress through the lesson.

The school principal (she/her) is a cisgender woman with approximately 20 years of experience; she has been a principal for the past 10 years but was a classroom teacher for about 10 years before that. After talking with Zoe about the challenges with disruptive behavior in the classroom, she got Zoe to agree that some additional training in classroom management would help Zoe experience more success with teaching. The principal has referred Zoe to the district's behavior support team for support with classroom management.

Darian (he/him) is a behavior specialist working at Mountain Creek School District. He is a Black cisgender man with about 15 years of experience consulting in the schools. He consults with teachers and families across the district in order to address behaviors of concern in the classroom. He has previously worked in behavior support as a paraprofessional and as a classroom teacher. Darian is a member of the behavior support team for Mountain Creek School District.

Mountain Creek Elementary School is a medium-sized elementary school serving approximately 450 students in grades K–5. There are about three classes per grade, and each classroom has around 25 students. The school has roughly 40% of the students receiving free and reduced lunch. Zoe would describe her classroom as "quite diverse," with the school zone containing a low-income apartment community, a domestic violence family shelter, and a wealthy gated community.

Intensive Needs Teleconsultation Referral

Estella (she/they) is a school psychologist contracting with a rural school district to provide teleconsultation services to support a special education teacher, Wendy (she/her), who works with a student on the autism spectrum, Nico (he/him). Estella has collaborated with this school district for 3 years; she supports students who receive special education services and need individualized assessment and intervention for behavior and mental health, all through teleconsultation. Administrators, educators, and caregivers in the district are familiar with the services that Estella provides.

Lakeside Elementary School is a small elementary school serving approximately 250 students in grades K–5. There are about two classes per grade, and each classroom has around 20 students. The school has roughly 60% of the students receiving free and reduced lunch. The students who attend this school live in a rural community in the southwest United States. The community is composed predominantly of White individuals, although there are many living in the community who are Latinx or Pacific Islander.

Estella is a Latine nonbinary person in her late 20s who speaks fluent Spanish and has worked as a school psychologist and behavior analyst for the past 5 years. She is from a middle-class background and continues to maintain that socioeconomic status with her professional career. Estella learned about teleconsultation in her graduate training through coursework, applied research, and practice; she pioneered these teleconsultation procedures in the current school district—and, as a result, Estella has provided access to much-needed services for many students within the district.

Wendy, the classroom teacher, is a White cisgender woman in her late 30s. She is from a middle-class background and continues to maintain that socioeconomic status as an educator. She has been teaching students on the autism spectrum for 15 years and is a committed and collaborative educator. Wendy requested support for her student Nico, regarding his ongoing property destruction that has been occurring throughout the first month of the school year. She tried prevention-based strategies by proactively removing items that he typically destroys; however, she is worried about creating an environment with limited enriching materials that are usually available in her classroom, and the impact of that on Nico and other students in the classroom. Wendy also tried reducing the frequency and difficulty of task demands; however, Nico continues to engage in property destruction.

Nico, the student client, is a 7-year-old Latinx child in the first grade. He lives with his biological Latinx parents (mother and father) and paternal grandmother in a heteronormative family that also includes an older sister who is in the fifth grade at the same school. Nico's family experiences poverty; however, his parents access social supports to help Nico in the community and at home. These supports include clinic-based applied behavior analysis services and small group community respite with peers. Nico's parents work multiple jobs to support their family, and despite their limited availability during school hours, they are very engaged with Nico's education and always arrange ways to attend school meetings. They also communicate with Wendy about Nico's daily progress and want to help as much as possible—they always try to support at home with positive behavioral strategies. In Nico's home, his family speaks Spanish; however, his parents communicate effectively with the school team in English, and when Nico attends school, he communicates using English, as well.

Nico has an educational classification of Autism and a community mental health diagnosis of autism spectrum disorder. He uses functional communication to request and label items, activities, and preferences; he also engages in some reciprocal conversations with adults and peers. However, he has difficulty with social communication, particularly social pragmatics and waiting for adult attention. Nico also experiences restrictive behaviors and interests around board games, which he enjoys playing with familiar peers and school staff. He tends to become anxious when interacting with new peers or adults. Nico attends classes in the general education environment for morning meeting, enrichment classes (art, music, PE), and lunch, and he receives his special education instruction around reading, writing, and math in his special education resource class with his teacher Wendy and her team of teacher support professionals. When he attends classes with his peers in the general education environment, a teacher support professional accompanies him and another student receiving special education services, in order to ensure that Nico and the peer are appropriately engaged in the content and as a resource for additional help.

3 RELATIONSHIP BUILDING DURING SCHOOL TELECONSULTATION

Beginning the teleconsultation process can be daunting, but teleconsultants should remember that the consultation experience they are about to embark on is very similar to in-person work—the relationship between the consultant and consultee is paramount to the successful outcome of the consultation process. Teleconsultants should prioritize building and maintaining relationships with consultees not only initially in the process but also ongoing throughout all stages of teleconsultation. The relationship, rapport, and working alliance are related terms that describe the interpersonal characteristics between the consultant and consultee (hereinafter referred to as *rapport*). These relational considerations are influential to the consultation process, namely due to the relationship between rapport and social influence. *Social influence* is the extent to which the consultant's interactions result in a desired change in the consultee's behavior (Erchul & Raven, 1997). Further, the consultation relationship is associated with successful consultative outcomes (Kratochwill et al., 2002; Leach, 2005).

Building rapport involves the process of consultees gradually perceiving consultative contexts (i.e., in-person and virtual spaces), consultation partners

---

https://doi.org/10.1037/0000366-003
Teleconsultation in Schools: A Guide to Collaborative Practice, by A. J. Fischer and B. S. Bloomfield
Copyright © 2024 by the American Psychological Association. All rights reserved.

(e.g., students, educators, caregivers), and consultation materials (e.g., data collection tools, documents, web apps) as valuable and reinforcing to engage (Lugo et al., 2017). This process occurs largely through interpersonal communication—verbal, written, and nonverbal behavior—and through telehealth, it can be harder to discern social cues via the online format (Jerome & Zaylor, 2000). There are, however, digital tools, strategies, and considerations for robust and dynamic virtual rapport building. In this chapter, we discuss applications of rapport building at different times in the teleconsultation process—before sessions, during sessions, and after sessions. Following the discussion of those applications, we identify strategies and tools to help problem solve and troubleshoot technology-related rapport-building barriers that can come up during the teleconsultation process.

RAPPORT BUILDING PRIOR TO VIRTUAL FACE-TO-FACE SESSIONS

The steps teleconsultants take to prepare for face-to-face synchronous sessions affect various aspects of the teleconsultation experience, which is similar to the initial rapport-building opportunities with your consultee(s) and student during in-person consultation. The following subsections describe how teleconsultants can strive for inclusive teleconsultation and equitable support, how they can arrange the physical and virtual environment, and strategies to initiate communication with consultees.

Striving for Inclusive Teleconsultation and Considerations for Equitable Support

School teleconsultants are not limited by in-state geographical boundaries, and for this reason, they might have the opportunity to support a variety of communities with teleconsultation practice. For school teleconsultants who are licensed to practice across states, their practice reach can expand to even more communities. School communities have much variability, both within and across school districts. As such, teleconsultants must consider the communities they serve, and differentiate their consultation rapport-building and engagement strategies based on the values and culture of each community. To understand community values, teleconsultants should spend time learning, reflecting, and discussing topics with school-community members, including partners at the school level and caregivers.

Teleconsultants should approach this process with humility, both initially and throughout the rapport building, while understanding that there is always new information to glean for ongoing experiences; our impressions of communities are dynamic and informed by individual histories, education access, and interactions within and across communities. A central aspect of understanding the community you serve is simultaneously understanding yourself, your history, your experiences, and the biases you bring to your practice, as well as how those considerations intersect with your current practice and actions taken to disrupt any behavior that could be harmful or exclusionary—teleconsultants should take purposeful steps to collaborate with consultees to create an equitable and inclusive teleconsultation context. Teleconsultants should engage in ongoing learning, be aware of biases from themselves and others, and commit to act in inclusive and equitable ways to support students. It is possible that forgoing these processes or viewing consultees' cultural identity and values as incompatible with or irrelevant to the teleconsultation process may inadvertently lead the consultant to provide less than optimal services (Fong et al., 2016). Brown and colleagues (2022) provided an excellent framework that teleconsultants can use to strive for inclusive consultation for diverse students (specifically centering the intersection of culturally, gender-, and sexually diverse students). This framework discusses the importance of creating a safe and supportive context for students who are marginalized due the intersection of their identities. The framework, which may serve as a reference for teleconsultants as they practice, describes five domains:

1. knowledge of gender- and sexually diverse issues
2. intersectional support of consultee learning and development
3. interaction of ethnically and racially minoritized, gender, and sexual orientation identities in school contexts
4. cultural variations in the consultation constellation
5. supporting consultee and student success

The first domain, *knowledge of gender- and sexually diverse issues*, involves the consultant deepening their understanding of gender- and sex-related issues as those issues relate to the consultant's own schema and how it affects the world around them. This is especially true for consultants from the dominant culture, who need to be aware that their culture is not neutrally positioned or unbiased against other cultures. The second domain, *intersectional support of consultee learning and development*, refers to necessary considerations to be made for training or development of consultees in regard to culturally, gender-, and sexually diverse affirming support. The third domain, *interaction of ethnically and racially minoritized, gender, and sexual orientation identities in school contexts*, takes the previous two domains and expands on gender- and sexually diverse identities within the school's social ecosystem, highlighting power imbalances that exist within this context.

The consultant's, student's, and consultee's cultural identities inform different interactions in the consultation process. Cultural variability in the consultation constellation exists, and teleconsultants should acknowledge the impact of individuals' cultures and lived experiences during the consultation process. The same is true in supporting consultee and student success. It is your responsibility to set up both the consultee and student to succeed, by matching communication styles and helping consultees challenge their own personal biases.

In addition to the Brown et al. (2022) inclusive consultation framework, Maheu et al. (2018) proposed a framework for improving telehealth competencies, which has direct relevance to teleconsultation. In that framework, they proposed telehealth cultural competencies related to digital literacy and effective communication practices. Teleconsultants should consider the potential impact of the consultee's preferred communication modality and style. When needed, you should explore the consultee's comfort with using a telehealth interpreter who is fluent in a specific language, so as to optimize the accessibility and collaborative nature of teleconsultation services. This consideration is particularly important for caregiver consultees who participate in the teleconsultation process. Further, the Coalition for Technology in Behavioral Science's framework for evidence-based Telebehavioral Health competencies lists "cultural competence" and "diversity" under Clinical Evaluation and Care, which is only one of the seven domains of Telebehavioral Health competence (Hilty et al., 2018).

Arranging the Teleconsultation Environment

Teleconsultants should consider certain logistics related to the teleconsultation experience, including aspects of teleconsultation that create connection between the consultant and consultee, as well as the physical arrangement of the in-person and virtual environments, in ways that are inviting and engaging. The same is true to consultees, and teleconsultants should be familiar with the nuances of arranging these environments, so that they can support the consultee with recommendations and troubleshooting during planning and times of uncertainty. However, considering the inequities that many of our students and their caregivers experience, an optimal learning space (e.g., stable; distraction free; well lit; access to clean water, food, and electricity) is not always available to them.

Community settings might be available, and if so, they provide opportunities for consultees to engage in optimized teleconsultation; you can recommend that students and caregivers use community settings such as public libraries or community centers with wireless internet access. When needed, you can help caregivers access those locations or collaborate with an educator or related service provider at the school level in order to support the student or caregiver. During teleconsultation, there may be instances in which the student and the consultee are in a living space (rather than school or community setting), which presents opportunities for breaches in privacy due to individuals other than the student or the consultee being in view of the camera (or out of view of the camera but able to overhear content discussed within the session). As such, teleconsultants should spend time discussing, with the consultee and the student, the potential breaches of privacy and confidentiality if sessions occur under these circumstances. Considering that teleconsultation services can occur in environments outside of the school setting (e.g., the student's living space, the caregiver's workspace), school teleconsultants need to implement purposeful, creative, and individualized relationship-building activities that maximize student engagement.

Optimizing the Experience

This section provides teleconsultants with useful information to help optimize the interpersonal interactions during teleconsultation and promote rapport through engagement and presence within synchronous videoconferencing sessions. Teleconsultants should keenly ensure that basic videoconferencing features are available—which include audio, video, and lighting—and that those features are functional and effective.

Audio

The availability of audio and related sound quality influence the experience for all individuals involved in teleconsultation sessions. At times, technical barriers such as audio feedback, echo, or inaudible sound can impede the quality and comfort of the experience. To ameliorate these concerns, teleconsultants should use headphones that have built-in microphones. Further, separate hardware for headphones and microphones works well as an alternative, and in some situations, having separate hardware (e.g., a free-standing microphone) allows for higher quality audio.

Video

Webcam quality varies in price and resolution (the number of pixels displayed on the screen), and teleconsultants should use a minimum of 720 pixels; however, higher resolutions, such as 1,080 pixels, substantively enhance the clarity of images. In addition to the webcam resolution, both the teleconsultant and the consultee should use the highest resolution display (i.e., monitor or screen) affordable/available. These displays are often integrated into a device such as a tablet, smartphone, or laptop, or as a separate display for a desktop computer.

Lighting

You should configure sources of lighting in such a way that the light emitted illuminates the front of the face, and when possible, go for natural lighting from windows. Additional lighting considerations include using multiple sources of lighting, a soft light tone, or tunable LED lighting. Using these features increases image quality, reduces shadows, and provides the consultee the opportunity to see the consultant as though they were in the same space. In contrast, without adequate lighting—and especially with backlighting—discerning facial features and nonverbal communication can be challenging. Also, backlighting can provide an ominous environment for your consultee, which could have undesired interpersonal implications due to the interrogative nature of the lighting. Commercially available ring lighting is a practical solution to provide robust lighting during teleconsultation.

Consultee access to lighting technology might be variable due to inherent costs associated with purchasing the equipment, and teleconsultants should mention these considerations in the initial rapport building and be extremely flexible if readily available lighting options are limited.

PROMOTING PRESENCE AND ENGAGEMENT

Central to the process of building rapport in the virtual space is the need to prioritize the presence of the teleconsultant as well as to promote engagement between the teleconsultant and consultee(s). Groom et al. (2021) defined "presence" in the context of telehealth nursing services, which they described as *telepresence*:

> Telepresence is the patient's, caregiver's, and clinician's experienced realism during a telehealth encounter that is created through connection and collaboration built on trust, support, and the clinician's skill at acting as the technology mediator when the third actor (technology) influences the patient or caregiver and clinician interaction. (p. 714)

The concept and application of telepresence, during school teleconsultation, are similar to other technology-mediated health services, such as nursing. In lieu of being present in the same space, teleconsultants can create higher levels of presence by intentionally applying engagement strategies in their practice, similar to a master educator who teaches in an online setting.

Teleconsultants can conceptualize "engagement" in the teleconsultation process similar to the way that educators engage students through online teaching and learning pedagogies. Online engagement is conceptualized as an investment, commitment, participation, or involvement in learning and consists of behavioral, emotional, and cognitive indicators (Fredricks et al., 2004; Henrie et al., 2015). Overall, when interacting with consultees or students, your strategies must be genuine and appropriately differentiated for the individual(s) with whom you are communicating. The following subsections describe considerations and practical tools that consultants can use to purposefully promote engagement and enhance presence through the teleconsultation experience. These include session duration and content, virtual backgrounds and effects, and videoconferencing settings.

Conduct Shorter and Targeted Sessions

Considering the impact of sustained virtual meetings and online interactions on the attention levels of teleconsultants, consultees, and students (i.e., Zoom fatigue), teleconsultants should be conscious of the phenomenon and create shorter, targeted sessions to maximize attention and engagement. We recommend that teleconsultation sessions last no longer than 30 minutes—which is a similar recommendation as for online teaching pedagogy, where instructors provide a brief break every 30 minutes (Fauville et al., 2021; Harvard University, n.d.). By conducting sessions of up to only 30 minutes, teleconsultants can keep the consultees and students (as needed) engaged in the session.

Virtual Backgrounds and Effects

When interacting through a virtual space, there are ways that consultants (and consultees and students) can customize their environment, virtually, to create a space that is inviting. Teleconsultants can use this feature to customize their background and personalize their environment to their consultee's or student's interests, or as a way that they can create a professional and engaging environment despite being in a space less inviting (e.g., a small office with many items). Some platforms allow interactive effects beyond the virtual background; these effects include blurring the background, various borders around the video frame, and virtual accessories (e.g., hats, glasses) and styling (e.g., lipstick, facial, eyebrows) that track the user's face. These tools are customizable to each user's preferences or can be omitted from the session. To use virtual backgrounds and effects, teleconsultants and their consultees or students need access to a computing device with an adequate graphics card.

Videoconferencing Settings

Teleconsultants should become familiar with the available videoconferencing software settings associated with their preferred platform, but also platforms that school districts and local education authorities use (e.g., Microsoft Teams, Google Meet, Zoom). Teleconsultants who competently understand various commercially available software packages can dynamically toggle settings, such as turning off/on the camera and muting/unmuting sound, as well as allow screen sharing permissions. We describe these features throughout the text in relation to their practical applications. Importantly, teleconsultants should be able to rapidly problem solve and support their consultees' interactions with these settings, which can help ease consultee uncertainty and maintain engagement.

INITIATING COMMUNICATION WITH THE CONSULTEE

When teleconsultants begin the teleconsultation process, they should initiate a connection with their consultee(s) through email. (Examples of these emails are embedded in the case studies at the end of this chapter.) This is an ideal time to introduce yourself and explain why you are reaching out and how you are looking forward to supporting the student(s) and the teacher through the consultation process. The initial correspondence with the consultee(s) should be customized to each consultation experience; however, with some information staying consistent across consultees and students, teleconsultants could have a templated introduction in text or create a linked video recording conveying that content. Other options include sharing a link to a professional website or professional social media page; however, teleconsultants should proceed with extreme caution when connecting with consultees on social media and make sure to (a) create separate accounts used exclusively for professional interactions and (b) never share personal accounts. Further, districts or agencies might have unique policies in place that limit social media use by staff—you should be aware of any parameters before using this communication modality.

Teleconsultants should also follow up with consultees as necessary, and if initial attempts through email are not successful, then teleconsultants should consider alternative forms of contact, such as a phone call or an in-person visit. If feasible, making an in-person visit can be useful for important conversations and building rapport, especially if there are other educators you are working with at the same school.

RAPPORT BUILDING DURING VIRTUAL FACE-TO-FACE SESSIONS

Once you have completed the presession rapport building and have received signed consent documents, you should prepare for an online face-to-face rapport-building session with the educator. You will also meet with the caregiver and student; however, the initial rapport building occurs with the educator. Having initial individual meetings with consultees and students allows for opportunities to speak candidly to everyone included in the teleconsultation process. You should keep in mind, throughout the rapport-building process, that the acceptability of technology for consultation has been shown to increase with exposure (Fischer et al., 2016); it might require time and repeated meetings to establish rapport. The following subsections describe in-session considerations for rapport building. The content is differentiated by discrete activities and strategies to use with educators, caregivers, and students.

Rapport Building With Caregivers and Educators

Building rapport with caregivers and educators is based on conversations and interactions that occur digitally, through email or synchronous videoconference. The educators and caregivers with whom you collaborate will be integral members of the team and critical to implementing interventions with the students you are all supporting. Because these school and family partners serve such an important role in the teleconsultation process, we need to ensure that they are engaged with the teleconsultant and the process overall so that we can adequately respond to student needs. When building rapport with caregivers and educators, teleconsultants should (a) prioritize intentionally establishing the relationship with consultees and exploring consultee interests and preferences; (b) discuss classroom and school context; (c) discuss positionality; and (d) establish roles, expectations, and responsibilities. Each of these areas is described in the following subsections.

Intentionally Establish Rapport

As teleconsultants begin and proceed through the teleconsultation process, a common theme of *intentionality*, or deliberativeness of the activities, will come up throughout this process. Unlike with in-person services, opportunities to have on-the-go conversations in the hallways or in the educators' lounge are less available. Also, with educators' busy schedules and competing professional demands, teleconsultants must take time to plan and thoughtfully build rapport throughout the experience. In the subsequent subsections, we describe how you can purposefully approach rapport building with consultees during teleconsultation by engaging in effective communication, showing mutual respect, and demonstrating shared trust.

Effective communication. A teleconsultant's ability to effectively navigate interactions with consultees is contingent on the teleconsultant's communication—how well they convey the content, in terms of both the substance of the conversation and the way the content is delivered. Because communication is the primary modality for rapport building in teleconsultation, teleconsultants need to embody effective social communication skills within the online environment. Strategies that teleconsultants can use to engage in effective communication include active listening, asking thoughtful questions related to the content, summarizing information, and checking for consultee understanding. Further, teleconsultants should avoid communication that is judgmental, while focusing on validating the consultee through the discourse. Teleconsultants can achieve this by respecting varying views, while conducting themselves in a compassionate and empathetic tone in writing and verbally. In addition to written and verbal communication, teleconsultants should also consider their gestures and other nonverbal communication—including purposeful eye contact with the camera (to simulate eye contact with the consultee), facial expressions, emphasizing head nods, and other affective indicators. You should also try not to engage in rapid-fire questions and to give ample time for consultees to respond.

Openness for questions and feedback. Teleconsultants should be poised for receiving questions and feedback from the consultee. You can also invite this type of communication from consultees by explicitly setting the expectation that the consultee will ask questions and provide feedback about the process and outcomes. The teleconsultant who creates a space for questions and feedback will create opportunities for collaboration and increase the likelihood that the consultee will reciprocate, throughout the teleconsultation process, when the teleconsultant is in turn providing feedback and asking questions. In Chapter 5, we discuss how teleconsultants can approach feedback to the consultee.

Use approachable language. The rhetoric that teleconsultants use during the teleconsultation process impacts how the consultee perceives and understands the information and subsequently implements procedures. You should prioritize language that benefits the consultee so they can easily comprehend the information while feeling comfortable to ask questions if any arise. As teleconsultants, we speak for the benefit of the consultee listener—and, therefore, our language should be approachable and relatable.

Set boundaries around communication. Teleconsultants should consider the parameters within which they are able to communicate with consultees. These considerations include communicating about when you are available (and when you are not), preferred ways of communication (e.g., text message, email, phone call, videoconference), and what the consultee can do if you are unavailable. By setting these boundaries during the initial rapport-building session with the consultee, you can approach communication through teleconsultation with confidence, knowing that you discussed these issues at the outset. Discussing these issues early in the teleconsultation relationship helps to align communication preferences, while establishing an understanding of the expectations around communicating.

Mutual respect. Establishing a reciprocal appreciation and respect between the teleconsultant and consultee(s) is foundational. We never want the consultee to feel as though we are condescending, patronizing, or demeaning in our interactions. Although, as a teleconsultant, you bring knowledge, skills, and experiences, the consultees also bring their own knowledge, skills, and experiences. We should acknowledge the consultee as the local expert of their student (or child) and clearly show that we value their contributions within the teleconsultation relationship. We also can communicate, to the consultee, that we are always learning and striving to understand (a) the student and the consultee and (b) the context in which the concerns occur.

Shared trust. A teleconsultant should also be aware of the consultee's previous experiences with consultation. You should ask the consultee about those previous experiences so that you can understand what worked, what did not work, and what they would have done differently. Consultees will also bring previous experience (or the lack thereof) with telehealth and working in teleconsultation (or consultation in general). As such, teleconsultants should discuss the teleconsultation format and give context to why you are conducting services through this format (e.g., COVID-19 pandemic related, shortage of providers locally). Further, explain to the consultee that you intend to follow through with all of the points and action items discussed, and remember that the consultation rapport is built on shared trust and that you want the consultee to be able to count on you throughout this process—and, likewise, you want to trust them in a similar capacity.

Explore Consultee Interests and Preferences

Teleconsultants should also spend time, during initial rapport building, learning about the consultees' preferences and interests. It is beneficial to ask consultees questions about what they do for self-care and well-being; what they enjoy when they are not teaching or supporting students; their favorite foods and snacks; and other family, community, activity, or social interests. When you understand the consultees' preferences for the aforementioned areas, you can use that knowledge to promote engagement by enhancing motivation.

Discuss Classroom and School Context

Teleconsultants should ask the consultee about their classroom and school context. Specifically, it will be helpful to have information on how the educator conducts their classroom, including positive behavior supports, social–emotional learning, and supports (e.g., calming corner). Further, teleconsultants should try to understand the school–community context, particularly the consultee's perception of the school culture related to support from other teachers, administration, and community partners (including parents). This is an approachable way for the teleconsultant to discuss content that is germane to the consultee's daily impressions, and they can weave in other rapport-building content while getting a sense of the school culture and context overall.

Discuss Positionality Within Consultation

The Maheu et al. (2018) framework discussed previously in this chapter (see the section on Striving for Inclusive Teleconsultation and Considerations for Equitable Support) also encourages teleconsultants and consultees to engage in ongoing conversations regarding their identity and positionality. Teleconsultants should include, specifically, a conversation about their positionality, how privileges and identity influence their experiences and learning history, and how that informs how they interact within their professional spaces. You can mention that you want to be culturally responsive in your consultative work and support the consultee's needs. You should also ask about your consultee's positionality and how it intersects with their role as caregiver, educator, or other partner who supports the student in the teleconsultation process. Our role is not to shame or judge, but to understand the context as comprehensively as possible.

Understanding this context can help you plan and respond to the intersectional needs and potential biases that can occur throughout teleconsultation. Incidents of implicit bias can occur, and having discussions about positionality at the outset of the teleconsultation process can create a space where both individuals can feel more comfortable to (a) respond to these incidents if they occur and (b) work collaboratively through the experiences. The following is an example of what a teleconsultant could say to facilitate this conversation: "While we work together, if you notice any of these situations, please bring them up with me; I see the feedback as an opportunity for personal and professional growth, and I value your insights as the classroom teacher."

Establish Roles, Explain Expectations, and Assign Responsibilities
As they build rapport with consultees, the final consideration for teleconsultants is to create a clear understanding of the roles, expectations, and responsibilities associated with the teleconsultation process. This is especially important as teleconsultants progress beyond the initial rapport-building activities. Teleconsultants should arrange the environment as clearly as possible at the beginning of the process and maintain throughout, which will help to prevent any uncertainty and increase consultee comfort and engagement. The following content describes how teleconsultants can engage in these steps in order to make parameters transparent for consultees.

Establish roles. The teleconsultant should be the administrative lead for the collaboration, but the consultee should have equal contribution in the relationship. Here we list each participant in the teleconsultation process and their associated roles:

- **consultant:** supports the consultee with knowledge and skills and ensures socially valid and effective interventions are implemented by the consultee to support the student
- **consultee:** supports the student through new knowledge and skills learned via the consultant and implements socially valid and effective interventions
- **student:** engages with socially valid and effective interventions implemented by the consultee

Explain expectations. The teleconsultant should discuss and clearly outline expectations for both the consultee and themselves. This is a helpful opportunity to solidify communication expectations and emphasize both your openness to feedback and your commitment to collaboration throughout the process. Additionally, remind the consultee of the positive intentionality toward the students, staff, and partners within the teleconsultation relationship and underscore that all members of the teleconsultation process are doing their best with the circumstances afforded.

TABLE 3.1. Example Responsibility Allocation Sheet

Responsibility	Participant		
	Consultant	Consultee	Student
Collaboration	✓	✓	
Initiate meetings	✓		
Scheduling	✓		
Communicate responsively	✓	✓	
Interact with teleconsultant		✓	✓
Implement intervention	✓		
Provide training and coaching		✓	
Collect data	✓	✓	
Provide performance feedback	✓	✓	
Receive performance feedback	✓	✓	
Meaningfully engage in curriculum			✓

Assign responsibilities. After teleconsultants and consultees have a clear understanding of the teleconsultation expectations, you should delve into anticipated teleconsultation responsibilities. It is helpful to record who will be accountable for different responsibilities and share that document with consultees so that they can reference the list of responsibilities. The types of responsibilities and partners included in the responsibilities document can be customized to the needs of the student/referral concern, and Table 3.1 shows an example of a responsibility matrix that teleconsultants would commonly assign. We also include a fillable example of this form in the online supplemental resources for this book (see the Responsibility Table at https://www.u-tteclab.com/book--text-resources.html).

Rapport Building With Students

During the teleconsultation process, teleconsultants should meet with students to build a relationship. Although students whom you support will vary in their abilities to allocate and sustain their attention, communicate, and navigate technology, you can meet each student where they are to engage synchronously through videoconferencing. School staff might need to facilitate the interactions for some students, whereas other students will be able to navigate the experience without adult support. Teleconsultants should ensure that they always have an on-site staff point of contact so that they can access assistance from school building staff if student support is required. Instances when a teleconsultant might need support include the following:

- when a student is engaging in disruptive behavior that poses a risk to themselves/others or destruction of property

- when a student is intentionally logging out of or turning off a device when they should not

Contextualize Yourself and Your Role

Begin the rapport-building experience with the student by contextualizing yourself and your role, specifically discussing how you plan to support the consultee and the student to be as successful as possible during the school day. Next, ask the student to describe themselves, their interests, and their preferred activities—this should resemble the initial rapport conversation with the consultee but be developmentally adapted for the student. You should use the information that the student provides to inform rapport-building activities, specifically targeting student engagement and positive shared experiences, which we discuss in detail in the following subsection.

Focus on Engagement and Shared Experiences

When working to build rapport with students, teleconsultants should prioritize engagement during synchronous videoconferencing sessions. Those sessions should focus on the student and the teleconsultant sharing experiences, particularly experiences that include student preferences. As with in-person classroom instruction, an effective way to build engagement with students through an online setting is to provide frequent opportunities for them to respond (Cuticelli et al., 2016; Sutherland et al., 2002). These opportunities to respond could include following strategies and applications in Table 3.2.

There are some caveats to consider with opportunities to respond. When you work with a student and share your screen, be aware of the content that you will be projecting. When visiting websites of interest to the student, and the content is unfamiliar to you, you should preview the material before sharing your screen with the student.

In addition to these opportunities to respond, you should enhance your gestures and nonverbal communication (e.g., head nods, waving goodbye at the end of a call), look at the camera to simulate direct eye contact with the student, and try to present yourself as more effusive than you would in person. When working with students, especially elementary school students, you might channel their favorite YouTube star or an engaging online educator. Although, as a teleconsultant, you do not provide direct therapy to students, you should still attempt to create a positive and supportive relationship with them. Table 3.3 lists strategies that teleconsultants can use

TABLE 3.2. Opportunities to Respond

Opportunity to respond	Application
Teleconsultant asks student question	Solicit direct information from student
Teleconsultant checks in with student about any questions or concerns	Create opportunity for student to inquire or share something that they are uncertain about
Teleconsultant asks student to type comments into the chat box/select a reaction icon	Create opportunity for student to share information or ask a question
Teleconsultant asks student to show a preferred toy, item, or book	Create opportunity to share an experience and learn about preferences
Teleconsultant asks student to update their virtual background	Create opportunities to ask student to customize their environment, similarly to consultees, and to help with comfort in the rapport-building process
Teleconsultant engages in an enjoyable activity through a virtual whiteboard	Create opportunity to collaborate or share experience that involves writing or drawing; can include games (e.g., tic-tac-toe)
Teleconsultant and student play a web-based game	Create opportunities for engagement; access online through paid and free game websites/software available
Teleconsultant shares a screen to browse images/videos	Provide opportunities to see and hear student's preferred content/interests
Teleconsultant uses online polling	Available within the videoconference platforms or separate web-based software (e.g., Mentimeter); gauges student preferences or solicits answers related to specific concepts or ideas

TABLE 3.3. Strategies and Tools to Increase Rapport

	Setting	
Strategy	Elementary	Secondary
Digital whiteboard	✓	✓
Online games	✓	✓
YouTube videos	✓*	✓*
Website browsing	✓*	✓*
Streaming music	✓*	✓*
Conversation	✓	✓

Note. Asterisk indicates that the teleconsultant should preview the content prior to sharing their screen with the student.

to build rapport with students, as well as suggested relevancy across elementary and secondary settings. Teleconsultants should differentiate their rapport-building activities and strategies when working with elementary or secondary students. Many of the same tools to deliver stay consistent; however, both the content discussed during the rapport-building session and the interaction style should match the developmental level and preference of the student. Teleconsultants should conduct online research on students' individual interests so that they can effectively incorporate these interests into the consultation process. If the student enjoys time with the teleconsultant during the rapport-building session, educators can consider incentivizing desired student behavior with time interacting with the teleconsultant.

MAINTAINING RAPPORT AFTER SESSIONS

External to the rapport building that occurs during synchronous teleconsultation sessions, the teleconsultant can also prioritize asynchronous opportunities to follow up with the consultee and the student. The teleconsultant can use email, text message, or a brief phone call (if the consultee prefers) to thank the consultee for taking the time to connect and share about their experiences. Especially during the intervention training and implementation stages of problem-solving teleconsultation, which we discuss in detail in Chapter 6, teleconsultants should consider providing thoughtful handwritten notes to their consultees, acknowledging implementation efforts, consultation success, or noticing their intentions and commitment to their work and appreciating it. To the extent available, affordable, and permitted, teleconsultants should consider sending or dropping off preferred snacks with consultees—as a token of appreciation or to share with their classroom staff. For example, after starting a new intervention with a student, the educator and their classroom staff might appear tired and somewhat discouraged. You could be responsive in this scenario by sending cookies out for delivery from a local, popular cookie store. We've found that being able to share preferred snacks with consultees helps build rapport and can be a useful strategy to maintain the consultation relationship. The idea of individuals coming together to break bread is universal and is helpful for facilitating social connection (Dunbar, 2017), and teleconsultants should consider using this strategy to enhance connection with their consultees. The following subsections describe ways you can maintain rapport, keep motivation up, and "follow up and follow through" with consultees and students.

Stay Connected With Consultees and Students

Your rapport-building work as a teleconsultant does not end at the conclusion of each session—rather, much of the rapport-building interaction and communication continues after the sessions wrap up, and through a variety of digital formats across the teleconsultation relationship. Teleconsultants should follow up with consultees through emails, text messages, applications such as Slack and Microsoft Teams (if you have established this as a communication channel), or any preferred modality. If using text-based communication, teleconsultants should consider obtaining a work device or Google Voice account so that they can set boundaries for communication on personal devices.

Because teleconsultants cannot easily have impromptu conversations with consultees, they should prioritize their ongoing communication with consultees and take initiative to reliably follow through. Many email services allow for the scheduling of messages to be sent at predetermined times, and teleconsultants should consider this feature to program in connection with the consultee, even with a brief weekly message checking in about progress or any questions. When staying connected with students, the teleconsultant should consider setting up a time each week for sharing experiences, touching base on progress, and even soliciting feedback.

Help Teleconsultants, Consultees, and Students Remain Motivated

Throughout the teleconsultation process, teleconsultants should anticipate variability in engagement, due to a variety of factors that the consultees (and students) may be experiencing in their personal and professional capacities (e.g., caring for a sick family member, conflict with a student's caregiver, living in shared living spaces). When you as a teleconsultant experience these variations in engagement with your consultees, refer to the initial meeting regarding conversations about values, intentions, and preferences for support. These conversations should be infused throughout the process but can help reorient the consultee to the goals if their engagement wanes.

You should continue to provide an optimistic and realistic outlook for support and try to motivate consultees in their work (i.e., improving fidelity of implementation), while recognizing their efforts and offering support. You can use motivational interviewing strategies to enhance the consultee's desire to engage in consultation behaviors that will be helpful to the student's overall progress. Teleconsultants interested in motivational interviewing strategies in consultation should refer to the commentary by Blom-Hoffman and Rose (2007) and seek professional learning to gain competency in these skills prior to using them with consultees. If motivational interviewing strategies are not effective and the consultee continues to be impacted by their circumstances, potentially showing signs of burnout, the teleconsultant should facilitate access to information, or referrals for support outside of the scope of teleconsultation (e.g., community mental health supports). It is important to note that bringing up referral options could be a sensitive subject to the consultee, and their response depends on their stigma and experience related to accessing mental health support.

Focusing on maintaining motivation, teleconsultants should also normalize virtual fatigue and take breaks and schedule well-being time to stretch, go to the bathroom, and eat a snack—especially in meetings that are longer than 30 minutes—and finish early when possible. Teleconsultants can always continue the conversation with the consultee at a later time or gather information asynchronously, but making sure a reliable communication channel exists is important with respect to more dynamic communication processes. You can also break up the videoconference meetings by using phones or other forms of communication, and you should mention that other options are available and that you are flexible with the modality (i.e., meeting through a nonvideoconference format is better than no meeting or discussion at all).

Maintaining motivation could be challenging for the teleconsultant, consultee, and student, and the teleconsultant should recognize barriers as they arise and work through those barriers collaboratively. In Chapter 8, we provide more information about navigating barriers during teleconsultation.

Follow Up and Follow Through With Your Consultees

Once consultee skills are initially maintained, teleconsultants should plan to follow up with consultees to check in after a predetermined period. This follow-up opportunity allows you to understand the durability of the intervention and its extended impact on student outcomes. Teleconsultants can provide ongoing feedback, if needed, as well as continue to maintain rapport. If as a teleconsultant you serve a community for multiple years, you will likely collaborate with some of the same educators on different occasions—and although supporting different students, teleconsultants will want to maintain those educator relationships so that you can rapidly start collaboration in the future. Being able to follow through in this way would happen organically in the hallways, but without being in those spaces in person, teleconsultants must program in time to touch base about anything needed. An email or brief text message is a great way to execute this follow-up.

Considering that the teleconsultation format does not afford teleconsultants the spontaneous chance to pass by the consultee in the hallway or educators' lounge, you must prioritize intentionality in following through with your commitments and expectations. When you say that you are going to do something, you should do it—use your reminder apps, take ample notes, and schedule emails to make it easier. Also, when setting up meetings, you should use digital calendar invites with videoconference links attached to the invite; this way, consultees have easy access to the link on the meeting day and time, and you can remain organized—it is mutually beneficial. In your follow-through, you should do as much as you can to reduce the consultee's effort needed to engage in the consultation process.

INTERPERSONAL CONSIDERATIONS DURING TELECONSULTATION

In addition to the technical considerations that impact rapport (described in detail in Chapter 8), there are also numerous interpersonal considerations that impact rapport building and maintenance during teleconsultation. You need to be interpersonally responsive to adapt to each of your consultees, especially because over telehealth there are some differences to in-person interactions. The following subsections describe ways in which you can optimize the interpersonal experience with the consultee.

Limiting Interruptions

During teleconsultation, give ample time for the consultee to finish speaking before you speak, and be particularly mindful of interjecting and interrupting while they are speaking. This is an ongoing consideration during the teleconsultation process, and if you do interrupt or interject, it is always okay to apologize and offer to the consultee to please continue with their description or comment. In the online space (and in person), you should always (a) be gracious with your ability to allow the other person to speak and (b) prioritize their engagement over your communication. Doing this can help create comfort, and you should interject only if necessary. You should use your social pragmatics of how and when you interject. You can benefit from having a list of the items that you need to cover and following up with the consultee regarding any questions left unanswered or unaddressed; you shouldn't feel as though you need to fit everything into the meeting time, as this is an ongoing experience. This is an important moment to highlight the need for boundaries in communication, and how prioritizing consultee engagement should not disregard the content—if the consultee is engaged in content that is tangential to the scope of the consultation goal, you should redirect their focus back to the student and supports; however, you should do so in a kind and patient style.

Consultee No-Show, Cancellation, and Session Avoidance

When you notice that the consultee frequently does not show up for scheduled meetings, cancels meetings at the last minute, or in general is avoidant of scheduling meetings, you should take active steps to help ameliorate any concerns around the teleconsultation process. You should remind yourself to set a positive intentionality and seek to understand why these situations might be coming up. Although there might be times when rapport within teleconsultation is impacted, many times these interpersonal considerations arise when educators are extremely busy with numerous competing demands—not necessarily anything personal with regard to you. If these issues arise, you should consider how you arrange the virtual environment and how you communicate, and you should prioritize ways to make it more likely for the consultees to attend and engage with you.

Slow Rapport Development

Meet consultees "where they are at," and make sure that you are aware of their previous consultation experiences. It takes time for a consultee to build rapport with a new teleconsultant, and not being present in the space could slow the rate at which rapport is built, even more than in person—especially if you are not using the strategies to build rapport that are outlined in this chapter. Consider a steady communication schedule and a focus on empowerment and validation in your interactions with the consultee.

Ruptured Rapport

Despite a teleconsultant's competency and the intentional efforts to establish and maintain rapport, ruptures in the relationship can occur. These ruptures may present as avoidance from the consultation experience or from interpersonal conflict between the teleconsultant and the consultee (Safran et al., 2011). In psychotherapy studies, a *rupture* is defined as a regression in the relationship between a therapist and client (O'Keeffe et al., 2020; Safran & Muran, 1996), which can result from disagreements about treatment goals or processes (Martin et al., 2000), interpersonal issues among consultation partners (Coutinho et al., 2011), or cultural differences (Gaztambide, 2012). To help mitigate this issue, you should continuously assess the status of the relationship between you and the consultee. You should remain aware of the words that you say, the tone of your voice, and your nonverbal expressions. This is especially important when your message content is related to performance feedback or a disagreement with the consultee. You should be aware of how you deliver messages and do your best to ensure that the consultee doesn't perceive them as being delivered out of frustration or discontent.

In addition to your own verbal and nonverbal behavior, you should remain aware of the consultee's demeanor and notice affective changes in facial expressions or body posture and attend to the consultee's level of engagement (e.g., does it look like they are multitasking?). Other situations that you should consider, and that could lead to ruptured rapport, include disagreements when selecting treatment goals or procedures, decreased treatment fidelity, and defensiveness considering mistakes (Safran et al., 1990).

Assessing and Repairing Rapport

Therapeutic ruptures may be overt or subtle, and—regardless of how they present—it is important to address them in a timely manner. Taylor et al. (2019) recommended that consultants (a) engage in candid conversations with their consultees and students to explore the behaviors that led to the ruptures and (b) apologize for mistakes, in order to rebuild the relationship. Overall, teleconsultants should be responsive to situations that arise; use appropriate humor and validation to bring levity to situations that can feel overwhelming to the consultee; and be approachable through vulnerability, authenticity, and empathy. Take the initiative to check in—and even just drop a line to say that you appreciate their work and efforts. Table 3.4 lists potential interpersonal considerations that we have discussed in this section and how teleconsultants can try to ameliorate those concerns during their practice.

Social Validity Considerations

You should assess for social validity throughout the rapport-building process. Understanding the consultee's and the student's acceptability and satisfaction with the teleconsultation process and outcomes will help inform how to address any barriers that arise. You should check in with the consultees and

TABLE 3.4. Strategies to Address Interpersonal Considerations During Teleconsultation

Interpersonal consideration	Mitigation strategy
Facial expressions	• Monitor facial expressions through the picture-in-picture display of the consultant video
Gestures	• Slightly exaggerate nonverbals to help emphasize communication
Eye contact	• Look at camera to simulate eye contact (or between head and camera)
Acceptability of teleconsultation	• Ask student/caregiver/educator what may be helpful to increase comfort • Reassure student that any initial discomfort with the technology will reduce with repeated exposure
Interruptions	• Apologize for interrupting, and always give the consultee the opportunity to speak
No-show	• Follow up with an email to reschedule • Try not to take the no-show personally
Cancellation	• Thank consultee for communicating the need to cancel, and reschedule the meeting
Slow rapport development	• Be patient and compassionate, yet persistent with slower rapport building with the consultee or student
Ruptured rapport	• Apologize for any factors that contributed to the rupture, or the consultee's perception of the rupture, and be open to feedback about how you might be able to repair the rapport

students often and throughout the teleconsultation process. Some domains you could inquire about pertain to the consultee's or the student's acceptability and satisfaction engaging, learning, and collaborating with the teleconsultant (or the plan developed for the student). Also, you should understand how the consultee is responding to potential distress, their perceived self-efficacy, and how you support those concerns if they arise. You can say things such as "I wanted to check in with you about the session I observed—I saw that the student was engaging in some difficult behavior, and I wanted to see how you are doing." Responding supportively to situations and soliciting feedback about social validity gives valuable contextual information and allows for opportunities to learn, grow, and respond effectively to any barriers or challenges that might occur within the teleconsultation context.

You should collect various sources of data to inform social validity about rapport, and these sources should include quantitative questionnaires and measures as well as open-ended qualitative content. Further, you should also gather information on social validity for both the process of consultation and the technology used within teleconsultation (e.g., assessing comfort with various technologies). When assessing the acceptability of the consultation process, teleconsultants should consider measures such as the Consultant Evaluation Form (Erchul, 1987), which is a measure to assess educator and caregiver satisfaction with the consultation supports, specifically the degree to which consultees found teleconsultants helpful. It is important to have comparison data related to the consultee's acceptability with the teleconsultation modality and the technology used within the process. Having this information can help discern barriers related to the technology-mediated service delivery compared to the consultation work. We recommend that teleconsultants assess the social validity of technology using the Technology Acceptance Model–Fast Form (Chin et al., 2008). This tool measures three constructs: usefulness, ease of use, and predicted usage. In Chapter 7, we provide a table with various social validity measures germane to consultation domains.

CASE STUDIES: RAPPORT BUILDING

Schoolwide Teleconsultation Referral

Mountain Creek School District's behavior support team received a referral from Mountain Creek Elementary School for teacher coaching of classwide behavior management strategies. The referral stated that the principal and the classroom teacher, Zoe,[1] met to discuss the challenges with disruptive behavior that Zoe had been experiencing in class. As Darian had previously worked with this principal and had experience regarding classwide and schoolwide interventions, he was assigned this referral.

First, Darian read the referral information, reviewed the school website, and looked up schoolwide data within the district's data management system. Before meeting with Zoe, he wanted to learn more about the school, her, and the students who were currently attending. Darian then drafted an email to her, introducing himself and inquiring about when they could meet, and closed the email with his phone number in order to give Zoe an alternative way to contact him if needed:

---

[1] All cases in this volume are fictitious.

To: Zoe@mountaincreek.edu
CC: principal@mountaincreek.edu
From: Darian@mountaincreek.edu
Subject: Behavior support

Hi Zoe,

My name is Darian, and I want to introduce myself. I am a member of the district behavior support team, and I have received a referral from you and your principal to discuss the challenges you've been experiencing in the classroom surrounding disruptive behavior during your lessons. That sounds really challenging to teach when you have students talking and getting out of their seats during the class. I've had some similar experiences when I was a classroom teacher and I want to work with you to help your class learn and have fun!

The first step would be for you and me to meet over a videocall to get to know each other a little better. From there, we will develop a plan together to provide some added support in your classroom. I can meet with you next Tuesday or Thursday during your morning planning period, or right after school on Monday. Would any of those times work for you? If not, please let me know some times that do. I have also provided my phone number below so that you can give me a call to schedule a time with you.

I look forward to collaborating with you over the next few weeks.

Talk soon,

Darian
Behavior Support Team
Mountain Creek School District
+1 555 555 1234

Zoe replied that Tuesday during her morning planning period was best for her to meet. After Zoe and Darian agreed on a time, he sent her and the principal a calendar invite with a link for the teleconsultation session.

Darian signed in to the teleconsultation session about 2 minutes early so that he would be prepared for when Zoe was able to join in. He knew that Zoe would be calling in right after her students had left to go to their physical education class, so she might be running behind; by signing in early, he made sure that he could be situated and ready whenever she was able to sit down to talk.

When Zoe signed in, the first thing Darian did was welcome her and introduce himself; he described his background and let her know that he was eager to work with her. He reviewed the scope of his services, as well as the consent process for working with Zoe and her classroom. Because Darian knew both the principal and the school from a previous referral, he shared with Zoe something that he knew about the school. He then asked her about her background and why she had become a teacher at Mountain Creek Elementary School. They realized that they had both gone to the same university for their degree in education. They continued to talk for 15 to 20 minutes about who they were, what their interests were, and what was important to them. Before Darian ended the call, they scheduled a follow-up time to gather more information about the referral and for Darian to observe in the classroom. Darian then emailed Zoe the consent forms and a summary of the next steps to begin working together.

Intensive Needs Teleconsultation Case

After Estella received the referral from Wendy's school principal, Estella started the teleconsultation process by sending a brief email introducing herself. In this email, she provided a rationale for consultation and inquired about a preferred time to meet through videoconference to start collaborating on the case:

> To: Wendy@lakeside.edu
> CC: principal@lakeside.edu
> From: Estella@lakeside.edu
> Subject: Behavior support
>
> Hi Wendy,
>
> My name is Estella, and I'm the behavior and mental health consultant for your district; I wanted to introduce myself as we begin working together this year. It's so nice to meet you—we haven't had the chance to connect yet, but I've worked with other teachers in the district and really look forward to our collaboration!
>
> As a member of the district behavior support team, the principal at your school presented a referral for a student in your class. I understand that you've tried many strategies to support this student this year, but you are seeking some additional support for the student. It sounds like the student is engaging in disruptive behavior, specifically throwing items throughout the day, and that behavior makes it hard for him to engage with the curriculum.
>
> The first step would be for you and me to meet over videoconference to get to know each other and discuss an overview of the teleconsultation process as we work together this year. I'm available to connect with you Wednesdays or Fridays during your morning planning period, or 2:00 p.m. on Tuesdays and Thursdays—the school counselor confirmed she can teach a social-emotional skills lesson to your students so you can step away. Would any of those times work with you? If not, please share some preferred times. I have also provided

my phone number below so you can give me a call or text to schedule a time with you.

I look forward to collaborating with you and your staff this year!

Estella
Behavior Support Team
Lakeside School District
+1 555 555 1818

Once Wendy confirmed the meeting time, Estella sent a calendar invitation with the videoconference link as well as a meeting link in the body of the email. Wendy and Estella met through videoconference at the designated time. Estella greeted Wendy and mentioned how great it was to connect and to support this case through teleconsultation. She explained that this meeting would be primarily to get to know each other and learn about Wendy's experience as an educator, Wendy's classroom, and the school community. Also, they used the initial rapport-building session to review and complete the consent process for Wendy.

After their 25-minute discussion, Wendy and Estella set a time to discuss the specifics of the behavior of concern during the problem identification interview. They also set up a time to observe the student when the behavior of concern was most likely to occur during the school day. Estella shared the Spanish version of the teleconsultation consent form with Wendy, and Wendy sent this form to Nico's caregivers in order to obtain their permission for Nico to participate in this process. Once Wendy received the signed consent form from Nico's parents, she informed Estella and set up a brief rapport-building session between Estella and Nico. Estella wanted to build rapport with Nico so that she could understand social and emotional skills. Because Nico highly preferred board games, Estella found a free digital board game online and played with Nico for about 30 minutes. Estella found this time with Nico to be very informative, and it helped her understand Nico in the context of the classroom and his preferred activities. She did not observe the throwing behavior during the rapport-building session. After completing the rapport-building sessions with Wendy and Nico, Estella documented these sessions in her electronic notes and prepared for the problem identification interview.

4 PROBLEM IDENTIFICATION DURING SCHOOL TELECONSULTATION

After building the initial rapport with the consultee, the teleconsultant should start exploring the nature of the concern or problem that the consultee would like to address. In problem-solving consultation, this is typically accomplished through a semistructured interview called the problem identification interview (PII; Kratochwill & Bergan, 1990). The PII is a crucial step within this framework—in fact, conducting an effective PII is highly related to overall achievement of consultation outcomes (Fischer et al., 2017). This is also relevant for teleconsultation services that adhere to the problem-solving teleconsultation model.

During the teleconsultation PII, you interact with the consultee through videoconferencing, which occurs face-to-face and synchronously. The teleconsultant uses this opportunity to gather relevant information about the consultee's concern. Specifically, you work with the consultee to operationally define the concern or problem, set up an initial data collection procedure and schedule, and plan for the remaining activities and expectations that will occur during the remaining problem-solving teleconsultation process. This interview is similar in content and structure to a high-quality functional

---

https://doi.org/10.1037/0000366-004
Teleconsultation in Schools: A Guide to Collaborative Practice, by A. J. Fischer and B. S. Bloomfield
Copyright © 2024 by the American Psychological Association. All rights reserved.

behavior assessment (FBA) interview. This chapter provides context to readers about the PII during teleconsultation.

PRIOR TO CONDUCTING THE PII

Teleconsultants should prepare for the synchronous PII session to efficiently navigate the experience for the consultee. Prior to the PII through teleconsultation, you should communicate with the consultee through the preferred modality (e.g., text message, email, communication app), in order to remind the consultee about the upcoming appointment. In the correspondence prior to the PII, you should also include a document with the PII questions that you intend to ask, so that the consultee has ample time to preview them. Although consultees might not have availability to thoroughly respond to the PII questions, providing access to them before the meeting creates an opportunity for the consultee to understand the scope of the PII. The correspondence between the teleconsultant and consultee should also include both a direct videoconference link in a text message or email and a videoconference link embedded in a calendar invite. Having redundancy in the videoconference link—meaning providing the link in different ways—creates more accessibility for the consultee and a greater likelihood of them engaging.

After communicating with the consultee, you should spend time preparing the materials that you intend to use during the PII. It can be helpful to create a folder—for each student and consultee—that includes infographics, graphs, data, and other resources, so that you can easily open those materials immediately before conducting the teleconsultation PII with the consultee. To help with efficiency, you can have those windows already open and minimized on the desktop so that the content is easily accessible.

Once all of the documents that you intend to share are prepared, you should also open some kind of software with which you can record notes during the PII. You may have a preferred software specifically made for documenting notes, or you may prefer simply using a new email window to document action items and notes throughout the PII session—which is a viable option, as are other straightforward modalities (e.g., word processor, spreadsheet). The important thing to remember is that note-taking digitally (rather than by hand) allows for increased efficiency, as you do not need to transpose written notes to digital records at the completion of the interview.

DURING THE PII

This interview translates well to the online space because synchronous video-conferencing means that the teleconsultant remains face-to-face with the consultee. The following information describes the specific questions that teleconsultants should ask during the PII.

Discuss Student Characteristics and Circumstances

First, gather information about the referral contexts and the key individuals involved. While much of the following text describes the process for discussing one student, the process is similar for individual, group, and schoolwide referrals. The teleconsultant should make every attempt to understand the individual characteristics of the student, as well as the unique circumstances that the student and their caregiver(s) experience. By understanding the student's unique context, teleconsultants can be responsive and strive for equitable practice with which to support the consultee and student. The student you support exists within an ecological framework, highlighting the intersection of the caregiver, school, and community. Taking a systemic approach to understanding the concerns the student or consultee experiences is important, especially as you account for the student's behavior of concern. Teleconsultants who take time during the rapport-building process to gather this context (we discuss this topic in Chapter 3) can take a "10,000-foot view" of the student concern. If you think that you lack this broader understanding and context, you should solicit this information from your consultees.

Define the Behavior

The teleconsultation process requires the teleconsultant to understand and operationally define the behavior that the consultee would like to change. This is typically achieved through identifying a target behavior to decrease and a replacement behavior to increase. These increases or decreases are typically demonstrated through reductions or improvements in the frequency, duration, or intensity of those behaviors. The definition of the behaviors that teleconsultants intend to increase and decrease should be observable and measurable, and we provide more context on behavior measurement later in this chapter. Most important, when defining the target behaviors, the teleconsultant and the consultee should ensure that the target behaviors and definitions are socially valid and culturally responsive.

Understand Antecedents and Consequences of the Behavior

After deciding on a target behavior, teleconsultants can gather information to contextualize it by understanding the immediate factors that evoke the behavior and the factors that maintain the behavior. These factors could be predictable events, people, or circumstances that occur immediately before (antecedent) or after (consequence) a student engages in a behavior. At times, these can be discrete or idiosyncratic; however, a careful analysis of these factors, through frequent recording of the antecedents and consequences surrounding a behavior, is helpful in understanding the immediate triggers and responses (see the ABC Data Collection Checklist and the ABC Data Collection Sheet online at https://www.u-tteclab.com/book--text-resources.html). When looking at this context within the antecedent–behavior–consequence (ABC) model data, you orient to the information by each target behavior—that way, you contextualize one behavior at a time. Later in this chapter, we discuss how to collect ABC data to help assess why the behavior is occurring. In Table 4.1, we provide definitions and examples of antecedents and consequences.

Understand Setting Events or Contextual Variables Related to the Behavior

Teleconsultants can also gather information to understand contextual factors that change the value of the reward (i.e., *setting events*; Wahler & Fox, 1981). It is important to note that setting events (commonly referred to as "motivating operations" in the applied behavior analysis literature; Nosik & Carr, 2015) can be confused with antecedents—which, we mentioned, trigger behavior. Setting events "set up" the likelihood of behavior (e.g., a student gets in an argument with a parent before school, and the student arrives at school irritable and withdrawn), while antecedents "set off" the behavior of concern. For example, when the teacher constructively asks the student to

TABLE 4.1. Antecedents and Consequences

	Term	
	Antecedent	Consequence
Definition	Trigger–occurs immediately before the behavior occurs	Response–occurs immediately after the behavior occurs
Examples	• A teacher instructs students to take out materials for an assignment.	• A teacher provides praise for working through a difficult assignment while staying calm.
	• A peer takes a preferred item from a student.	• After the student yells that they are going to tell the teacher, the peer gives the item back.

correct an error (i.e., antecedent or trigger), the student yells at the teacher (i.e., behavior) because the student is still experiencing agitation from the argument with their parents earlier that morning. In Table 4.2, we provide a definition and examples of setting events.

Create a Plan for Data Collection and Progress Monitoring

Teleconsultants should collect similar data as you would in person; however, when collecting data remotely, consider the ways in which you collect those data. You should present consultees with the opportunity to integrate digital surveys and measures, through web-based apps, in their practice. Additionally, you should share a secure cloud storage folder to easily transfer information between all partners. Data sharing and progress monitoring should occur through a digital format that allows for convenient visualization and analysis of those data, ultimately allowing for responsive treatment changes and decisions about maintenance, generalization, and need for changes. Fortunately, schools should have institutional access to secure cloud storage platforms that teleconsultants and consultees can use to share data. Some examples of data collection methods are listed following, and Table 4.3 provides additional information regarding specific applications for using the following measurement options:

- ABC data (Ikeda et al., 2002)
- systematic direct observations (Hintze et al., 2002)
- direct behavior ratings (Chafouleas et al., 2010)
- scatterplots (Delgado et al., 2017)
- permanent products (Sanetti & Collier-Meek, 2014)

TABLE 4.2. Setting Events

	Setting events
Definition	Environmental events that have an indirect impact on behavior. They momentarily change the value of the reward or punishment associated with the behavior, therefore either increasing or decreasing the likelihood that the behavior will occur. They can be removed in time or occur simultaneously with the antecedent.
Examples	• A student did not have ample sleep, did not eat breakfast, or had an argument with a caregiver or peer prior to attending school.
	• A student experienced bullying at recess prior to instruction on a difficult content area.
	• A student did not take a prescribed medication.

TABLE 4.3. Data Collection Methods and Applications

Data collection method	Teleconsultation application	Example digital data collection tools
ABC data	Understand the triggers and responses to problem behavior.	Autocalculating ABC Data Collection Sheet (see the online supplemental resources at https://www.u-tteclab.com/book--text-resources.html)
Systematic direct observations	Take note of variability of student behavior over a short, sampled amount of time.	Data collection apps such as BehaviorSnap, Behavior Observation Made Easy, or LiveSchool
Direct behavior ratings	Rate student behavior on a set scale over a sample amount of time.	DBR forms available online at (https://dbr.education.uconn.edu/)
Scatterplots	Correlate behaviors to specific times that they occur in a natural setting.	Copying data from Google Sheets or Excel into Visme or Canva for a user-friendly scatterplotting experience
Permanent products	Collect physical indicators of an implemented intervention through a student's work.	PowerSchool, Canvas, Schoolytics, or any school information system that can be used to analyze permanent products
		Behavior Tracker Pro to record video of products of specific behaviors in real time

Note. ABC = antecedent–behavior–consequence; DBR = direct behavior ratings.

ABC recordings function to identify the association between various contexts, antecedents, and consequences of behavior. Checklists can serve as efficient methods to record occurrences of problem behavior by having the teacher (or whichever adult is with the student) record start/end times and check off the context, preceding events, and resulting consequences. Direct behavior ratings are an accessible and acceptable form of data collection that allows consultees to collect data based on the occurrence. Scatterplots seek to identify patterns related to problem behaviors and specific time periods; adults record in which time slot the problem behavior occurred. Systematic direct observations, on the other hand, may require momentary time-sampling in which you note the student's behavior (e.g., disruption, academic engagement, inattention) at the end of 15-second intervals across a 20-minute observation period. To the extent possible, you should collect data using permanent products, which are lasting artifacts showing that the intervention was implemented. Teleconsultants can refer back to the permanent products to monitor student progress related to the intervention.

If synchronous observation opportunities are not available, teleconsultants should consider training consultees how to record data or video samples, which consultees can upload to a secure cloud storage folder for convenient reviewing and coding by the teleconsultant. Additional consent procedures are required for all students and educators who appear on recordings, and appropriate consent and assent procedures should be conducted accordingly.

The advancement of technology has resulted in a variety of options for developing data collection tools. For example, depending on your familiarity with technology and experience with data collection, you can design and use paper-based data collection sheets (see the ABC Data Collection Checklist in the online resources at https://www.u-tteclab.com/book--text-resources.html) or an Excel data collection tool that will automatically convert analyzed data into graphs or other figures. Regardless of the type of data collection tool, it is important that it includes areas for recording dimensions of target behaviors (e.g., frequency, duration, latency, intensity) and other information related to the context in which a behavior occurs (e.g., date, setting, stage). Consultees may endorse different levels of experience with data collection, so you should accommodate this by providing training and examples prior to data collection, as well as codesigning easy-to-use data collection procedures.

AFTER THE PII

After completing the PII through teleconsultation, you should document the session—concisely yet informatively. If you have limited availability to document notes, you should consider using a dictation feature to orally describe the session in a secure web-based document. You can save the dictated content, and at a convenient time, you can edit it and include it in a more formal written note. Next, you should follow up with the consultee through an email. In this follow-up email, provide a brief, written summary of the information gleaned from the meeting, as well as any relevant action items for the consultee. Action items for consultees might include familiarizing themselves with measures for baseline data collection (and beginning collecting data), sharing student records, or connecting the teleconsultant with a student's caregivers.

Finally, teleconsultants should ensure that consultees collect data and share those data regularly. Teleconsultants also should make sure that ongoing progress monitoring is established and conducted reliably. As we mentioned in Chapter 3, progress monitoring the target behaviors could be the responsibility of either the teleconsultant or the consultee, and, to the extent feasible, teleconsultants should consider digital data collection modalities. There are some unique ways to progress monitor data through digital modalities; for example, Radley et al. (2016) used a decibel meter for noise reduction within a classroom. Considering the different ways that teleconsultants and consultees can collect data, you should familiarize yourself with the content in the subsequent sections of this chapter in order to help inform which data collection methods you use.

FUNCTIONAL BEHAVIOR ASSESSMENT

The synthesis of the information and data collected through the PII process will inform an FBA (O'Neill et al., 2015). The FBA is a procedure that you can use to understand the contextual factors that maintain behaviors of concern (i.e., the function of the behavior), and that assessment can be used to develop a function-based intervention plan to support the student. Behavior concerns are often challenging and can be stressful to manage, particularly in the classroom. When students engage in such behavior, however, there is often a purpose—they are trying to communicate. An FBA is an individualized problem-solving process that involves collecting information about the environmental conditions that precede the problem behavior (i.e., antecedents) and the events that occur afterward, which reinforce the behavior (i.e., consequences). The Individuals With Disabilities Education Act (2004) requires that FBAs must be conducted when

- a student with a disability has been removed from school for more than 10 cumulative school days, and the misconduct is determined to be a manifestation of the student's disability

- the parents object to a change in placement or additional suspension time

- the student with a disability has committed a safe-school violation

- the general components of a comprehensive FBA include (a) identifying problem behavior; (b) describing the problem behavior in objective terms; (c) measuring the magnitude of said behavior; (d) identifying the antecedent, individual, and consequence variables that influence the occurrence of the behavior; (e) the function of the behavior has been hypothesized; and (f) the FBA contributed to a function-based intervention to address said behavior (Steege et al., 2019).

Although these are requirements for when an FBA must be completed, we recommend that you conduct some variation of an FBA in order to inform your services, especially at the targeted (Tier 2) and individual (Tier 3) levels. The following subsections describe the types of FBAs that you can use during your practice, as well as the process for conducting FBAs.

Types of FBAs

There are two commonly used types of FBAs in school teleconsultation: indirect and descriptive methods. (We discuss a third behavior assessment method, experimental functional analysis, in Chapter 5.) In this section, we provide a summary table (see Table 4.4) and share additional information regarding the scope of each of these types of FBAs.

Indirect FBA

Indirect data collection methods include reviewing existing behavioral records (e.g., office discipline referrals); using behavioral checklists and/or rating scales; and conducting interviews with educators, caregivers, and the student in order to provide insight as to why the behavior occurs. Function-based interviews help provide further information about the conditions that prompt and reinforce the behavior. The Open-Ended Functional Assessment Interview (Hanley, 2012) is an example, asking questions that focus on an objective description of the behavior (e.g., "What does it look like?"), potential antecedents and consequences (e.g., "How do you and others react to the problem behavior?"), and possible behavior functions (e.g., "Why do you think they are engaging in the problem behavior?"). In contrast, the Questions About Behavioral Function form is a closed-ended Likert-type

TABLE 4.4. Data Sources for Functional Behavior Assessments (FBAs)

	Type of FBA	
Data source	Indirect	Descriptive
Interviews with educators and caregivers	✓	
Record review	✓	
Surveys or questionnaires	✓	
Direct observation		✓
ABC data		✓
Rating scales		✓

Note. ABC = antecedent-behavior-consequence.

scale that requires raters to determine the frequency of certain behavior functions (Paclawskyj et al., 2000). At the conclusion of rating each item, responses are integrated and reveal the most likely behavior function (i.e., attention, escape, nonsocial, physical, and tangible).

Descriptive FBA

Descriptive methods of data collection differ from indirect methods in that they include the direct observation of the student in the environment in which the behavior reportedly occurs. This type of assessment requires observation and documentation of antecedents, behaviors, and/or resulting consequences. Four ways to conduct a descriptive FBA are by using (a) ABC data collection, (b) scatterplots, (c) systematic direct observations, and (d) direct behavior ratings. Teleconsultants should use a variety of these descriptive measures to inform their FBA. For further information about descriptive FBA procedures, consult a text on the FBA process, such as Steege and colleagues (2019) or O'Neill and colleagues (2015).

The FBA Process

The process for conducting an FBA is not necessarily defined by federal law, and the standards for FBAs differ across local education authorities. Additionally, each local education authority likely follows a unique procedure for the FBA, and teleconsultants should understand what that process looks like, so that they adhere to those standards for each student that they support. Despite procedural variability across school districts, we provide a standard overview of the process, and you can use this outline as an example of the referral and FBA process.

First, the behavior consultants (or "behavior team") receive a referral. The consultants ensure that classroom management strategies are established and maintained. They also ensure that the teacher has attempted some targeted intervention strategies with fidelity before beginning FBA procedures. Once the initial interventions are analyzed, indirect FBA methods are used. These include the use of open-ended FBA forms, questions about behavior function (or other related questionnaires), and a review of student academic and behavior records (e.g., office discipline referrals). Next, descriptive FBA methods are employed, including direct observations (e.g., systematic direct observations [at least three]) and teacher-conducted ABC data collection for at least 2 weeks. When all of the data have been compiled, a full FBA report is completed. The FBA report includes an operationally defined problem behavior, relevant setting events (e.g., insufficient sleep) or previously attempted interventions, observed antecedents and consequences, a hypothesized function, and function-related recommendations. The FBA report is used to inform the development of an individualized behavior intervention plan.

Informing Function-Based Interventions

At the conclusion of the FBA, results should inform potential interventions or supports that match the hypothesized behavioral function. When crafting the plan, it is important to do the following:

- provide a clear overview of the problem and include all relevant details
- include replacement (alternative) behaviors for the student to engage in
- include information and resources for data collection
- include explicit instructions and information regarding training, implementation steps, and individuals who will participate
- provide antecedent and consequence strategies
- maximize reinforcement and minimize punishment procedures

In Chapter 5, we discuss the problem analysis stage and provide further information related to the conceptualization of the intervention, based on the data collected during the problem identification and problem analysis stages.

PROBLEM SOLVING DURING THE PROBLEM IDENTIFICATION STAGE

During the problem identification stage, teleconsultants will need to attend to issues that arise, and these issues can be similar to the concerns that they experience during in-person services. Although we discuss some of the broad barriers to teleconsultation in Chapter 8, the concerns during the problem identification stage could arise in the other problem-solving teleconsultation stages, as well.

If a teleconsultant experiences a poor internet connection, cannot access the internet, or has the videoconference dropped, they should switch to a phone call. This will allow the consultee and teleconsultant to pick back up with the conversation and not get inundated with the task of trying to reestablish the internet connection of the device. As we mentioned in Chapter 3, maintaining the momentum with consultee engagement is critical in the teleconsultation process, especially early on.

Teleconsultants might experience issues scheduling meetings, especially when multiple consultees are involved in the process. To support scheduling, consider using scheduling applications or find a preferred time for the individual with the most constrained schedule and work around their availability. Making sure that all of the relevant partners attend these meetings is influential to the student's overall success, and taking the initiative to schedule and plan meetings will help guide the teleconsultation process.

Throughout the problem identification stage, you might notice a consultee's gap in knowledge or skills, which could lead to a misunderstanding of the student or system. As teleconsultants, it is important to take a constructive approach and support learning and developing new skills to empower the way we arrange the environment for students. Particularly at the problem identification stage, discrepancies might arise related to deciding on a target behavior or the contextual factors that influence the behavior. When this occurs, you can verify the context through digital observations of the student in their academic setting. In the next section, we discuss this topic as it relates to social validity.

SOCIAL VALIDITY DURING THE PROBLEM IDENTIFICATION STAGE

The same as with in-person consultation, teleconsultants need to verify the behavior of concern through direct observation of the student and ensure that they are creating an intervention that results in meaningful changes for the student—and that is informed by student participation to the extent possible. You can provide an objective perspective around the behavior of concern, help refine the definition of the behavior, and help set meaningful goals. Even though, as teleconsultants, we strive for objectivity in our work, it is important to check our biases throughout the process and make sure that we are addressing a referral in a way that results in a positive and meaningful educational benefit for the student.

CASE STUDIES: PROBLEM IDENTIFICATION

Schoolwide Teleconsultation Referral

During the second meeting with Zoe, Darian conducted the PII to gather more information about the challenges that she was reporting in her classroom. Zoe described how her class had been acting out a lot that year: Students were getting out of their seats, calling out, talking to their friends, and playing on their phones during class. Zoe said that she was finding it difficult to finish all of her lessons, and she reported that she was having to frequently stop the lessons in order to redirect the class and address behaviors of concern.

Darian asked Zoe to describe some of the strengths of her class that year, as well as some of the activities that the students seemed to like the most. Zoe noted that the classmates seemed to get along with each other overall. None of the enrichment teachers and substitutes had reported any major incidents, and they had found the students to be mostly respectful yet talkative. While Zoe had some students who had been struggling academically, the majority seemed to be learning the concepts that semester.

Darian then asked some more about when the challenges would occur and what Zoe typically would do in response. The afternoons seemed to be the hardest time for the class, and Zoe had noticed that it was especially challenging around a long weekend or school holiday. She had previously tried taking away recess and calling home, but that had not seemed to have made a difference. She now frequently would send students down to the main office to meet with the principal. When certain students, whom Zoe called the "ringleaders," were not around, she could get through most of the lesson. However, once any of her students were off task, it was difficult to get them back on track.

After gathering relevant information about the context of when the class was most disruptive and strategies that Zoe had tried in order to address these concerns, Darian wanted to summarize what she had reported thus far and then identify a definition of the target behavior:

> Let me make sure I have this right: Although your class is mostly *respectful* and well liked, they have been *acting out* a lot during your lessons. You see them get out of their chairs, walk around the room, and talk to one another when you are trying to teach. After lunch and recess is the hardest, and it's particularly tricky around long weekends. While sending some students to the office has helped you get back on track, it hasn't necessarily solved the problem. How is this sounding so far?

After Zoe agreed to the summary, Darian defined the target behavior in a measurable way and discussed data collection with her. The next step after this meeting will be for Zoe to start collecting some data about how often the behaviors occur. Because Zoe and Darian want to focus on a positive target behavior, their target outcome will be academic engagement, or on-task rate. To have a simple data measurement plan, Darian has asked her to capture, throughout the day, the number of students on-task at preset intervals. This data collection system will be a PLACHECK, or Planned Activity Check. At each interval, Zoe will count how many students are sitting in their chairs, looking at either the instructional materials or the teacher and not talking with peers. She will note, on the data sheet that Darian will provide, the time, the activity, and the number of students. Every day after school, Zoe will email Darian the summary sheet of the day; in a week, they will meet to review that cumulative data.

Intensive Needs Teleconsultation Referral

After the initial rapport-building sessions, the teleconsultant, Estella, and the educator, Wendy, planned to meet to discuss the student concern and gather additional information to support the plan conceptualization. Estella emailed Wendy 1 day prior to the meeting to remind her of it, provide the link to it, and supply her with a list of some of the questions they would discuss. Wendy appreciated having these questions so that she could browse the content before connecting with Estella.

Once Wendy joined the meeting with Estella, Estella greeted her and asked how she had been doing since they last connected. After initial greetings were exchanged, Estella reviewed the purpose of their meeting, which was to understand why Nico's behavior was occurring; during the meeting, they would be going through the problem identification questions that Estella had sent through email. Estella shared her screen with Wendy so that they both could read the questions as Estella asked them. Through the problem identification interview, Wendy and Estella established the behavior of concern as "property destruction"—which they operationally defined as breaking pencils and ripping up academic materials. The property destruction was accompanied by Nico complaining about the work being too hard and saying that he needed help from the staff. Wendy explained that she and her teacher support professionals had noticed that Nico's property destruction and complaining were happening across all class subjects and activities and that the behavior tended to occur when the educators were busy supporting other students. Wendy communicated that she and her staff tended to attend to Nico after he engaged in property destruction and that they would like to figure out ways to proactively address these problems so that they didn't have to take up too much time responding to these issues throughout the day. Wendy said that she and her staff would prefer Nico to work through assignments independently and to request help only when he actually needed it—especially when they were supporting other students in the classroom.

Estella discussed with Wendy options for initial data collection for the behavior of concern, and they decided to collect ABC data and a daily frequency count of the occurrence of property destruction. They also planned to collect data on the occurrence of Nico complaining about work difficulty, so that they could understand the relationship between the property destruction and the complaining. They agreed to collect these data daily for 2 weeks. Estella mentioned that during that period she would virtually visit Wendy's classroom three times to observe the student during group learning—which was when Nico seemed to engage in the problem behavior most often. Estella also told Wendy that she would text her the morning of the observation and again 15 minutes before the planned observation time, as reminders to make sure the technology was functioning so that Estella could virtually join the classroom and conduct her systematic direct observation of the behavior of concern.

After conducting the digital observations in Wendy's class, Estella connected with Wendy through email to set up the problem analysis interview, discuss the results of the data collection, and collaborate on a plan to support Nico. Estella also invited Nico's parents to join this meeting so that they could hear about the information that had been gathered and collaborate through the process.

5 PROBLEM ANALYSIS DURING SCHOOL TELECONSULTATION

The next step in the problem-solving process is the problem analysis stage. During this stage, the consultant analyzes the information collected during the problem identification interview (PII) and then reviews that information with the consultee and jointly determines a plan to best address the referral concern. Part of this process includes a semistructured interview called the Problem Analysis Interview (PAI). This step is crucial to the problem-solving consultation process in that the information collected helps set the baseline measure for success.

During the PAI, as well as for the other forms of data collection, you will interact with the consultee, observe the client, and communicate with other members of the team through various forms of technology, including videoconferencing, phone calls, email, and online questionnaires. This process parallels the functional behavior assessment (FBA) process in that you are reviewing relevant information to be able to design an individualized intervention plan that is ecologically valid, effective, and feasible in the classroom. All of the information collected at this stage of the teleconsultation process is to support treatment planning and then for future evaluation of

---

https://doi.org/10.1037/0000366-005
Teleconsultation in Schools: A Guide to Collaborative Practice, by A. J. Fischer and B. S. Bloomfield
Copyright © 2024 by the American Psychological Association. All rights reserved.

the effectiveness of the intervention plan. This chapter provides an overview of the PAI conducted over teleconsultation, methods to collect data using technology, and some data collection examples adapted for teleconsultation.

PRIOR TO CONDUCTING THE PAI

Following the PII, the consultee collects some antecedent–behavior–consequence (ABC) data to understand the relevant antecedents and consequences of the target behavior. This is necessary to help determine a hypothesis of the function of the behavior. In other words, what is the student communicating with their behavior of concern? The problem analysis stage involves the consultant and the consultee reviewing the data collected, as well as other relevant information that they have previously collected relating to this student. That may include previous evaluations, work samples, grades, attendance, and behavior referral records. The consultant will use all of this information to inform the PAI. The consultant is analyzing whether the student's behavior is related to an unmet need or lagging skill, so that the treatment plan can be aligned to that need, as well as explicitly teaching the skill so that the student is more successful in the classroom.

With the information gathered previously, the consultant and the consultee are seeking to assess whether the data collected align with the referral description. There are times when the data collected show that the behavior of concern is less severe or less frequent than initially described. For example, the teacher could have referred a student for disruptive behavior in the classroom, yet the data collected show that the target student's rate of disruptive behavior during lessons is comparable to those of the other students in the class. As a result, the consultant can discuss with the consultee about a change of target: The whole class might be a better target for intervention, or the initial referral concern could be changed.

One form of data frequently used with individual student referrals is ABC data collection. In this, the consultees have been collecting information on the antecedents and consequences of the target behavior. When done with high fidelity, the consultant can also review the frequency of the behavior of concern. The consultant would then review the data and develop graphic displays to summarize common patterns in the behavior of concern. Traditionally, these data are collected with paper-and-pencil data sheets. The consultant may use a digital form, which can expedite the data analysis process. A digital form can automatically summarize the data and allow for seamless graph creation, saving significant time for the consultant. For example, the student might display the behavior at a much higher rate during math instruction than

FIGURE 5.1. Example Bar Graph: Frequency of Target Behavior

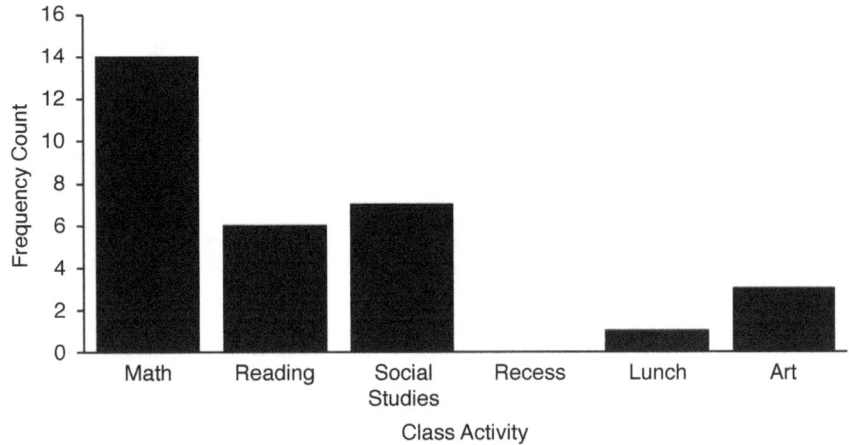

during lunch or recess (see Figure 5.1). A bar graph of settings for the behavior would quickly show this to the consultees during the PAI.

For classwide and schoolwide referrals, the consultant can review the office referrals, grades, and attendance data. Much of these data are already collected, and the consultee can easily share this information with the consultant. While individualized ABC data might not be appropriate for a group or systems-level referral, the consultant can go about the same process of gathering data, analyzing for patterns of behavior, and developing a plan in partnership with the consultee. When the information is shared with the consultant, the consultant can develop visualizations that will help the consultant communicate patterns in the data. Similar to the graph for the ABC data described previously, the consultant can show a graph of behavior incidents in the classroom by activity. This could show that there is a higher rate of behavior incidents during whole-class instruction than independent seatwork (see Figure 5.2). Similarly, the rate of academic engagement can be presented by type of classroom activity.

DURING THE PAI

The PAI during teleconsultation is a semistructured interview during which the consultant and consultee(s) meet over videoconferencing to discuss the data collected, finalize the referral concern, and begin to develop a treatment plan. All relevant partners—including the educators, caregivers, other school personnel, and sometimes the student themselves—are in attendance

FIGURE 5.2. Example Line Graph: Rate of Behavior Incidents by Activity Type

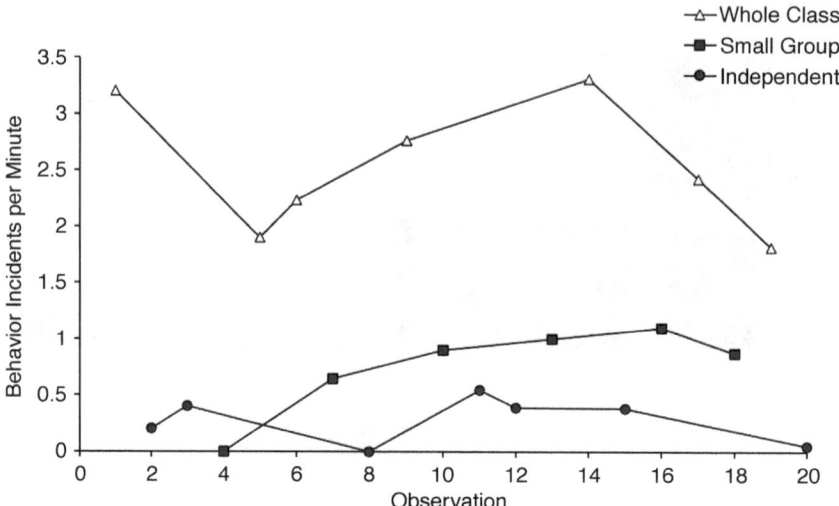

to review the information. Prior to the teleconsultation meeting, the consultant will collate all data collected; store the information in a clear, easy-to-locate folder; and develop some visualizations for the data to review. The consultant can create a shared cloud-based storage folder for the consultee(s) to upload data they have collected, which would easily allow the consultant to see the data in real time, as well as facilitate data analysis.

Once the data have been collected and stored in a shared location, and graphic visualizations have been created, the consultant will note some additional questions or information needed that they can collect during the PAI. This will be helpful during the joint interview with the consultant, consultee, and other relevant partners.

Review Data

The initial part of the PAI is to review the previously collected data. During this time, the consultant is validating any concerns, and the team is identifying the significance of the referral concern. There are times at this stage that the review of data may indicate that the referral is not as significant as initially thought, and the team will either terminate teleconsultation services or modify the referral.

The consultant will be sharing the data visualizations that were developed with the team during the videoconference, describing patterns in the data, and asking follow-up questions. By using screen sharing features of the videoconferencing platform, all participants can have equal viewing of the data. To improve the quality of the demonstration, the consultant can use annotation features to highlight or draw attention to certain features of the data while discussing. For example, when reporting that the student engages in the behavior at a higher rate during math instruction, the cursor can point to that bar to better describe the data to all observers. Similarly, if the consultant used any video observations of the target student to gather this initial data, the consultant can use photo and video clips of the target behavior to provide examples to further describe the data.

At this time, the consultant may have additional questions or seek to gather additional information to support hypothesis formation. This can proceed as an interview or discussion with the participating members of the meeting. If there are any disagreements or confusions, you will assess the provided information and obtain clarification from all participating parties.

Discuss Behavior Function

After summarizing the data, the teleconsultant, in collaboration with the consultees, will review the definition of the target behavior, summarize the antecedents and consequences of the behavior, and develop a summary statement of the function of the target behavior. This process is similar for individual, group, or schoolwide referrals; in all cases, you want to identify shared language to describe the target behavior and come to an agreement on the function the behavior serves. That shared understanding will best support plan development regarding the skills to teach and the changes to the environment that the consultee can enact in order to best address the referral. At this point, the definition of the target behavior was identified during the PII and may only require minor modifications.

At this point in the discussion during the PAI, the team will identify the hypothesized function, or reason why someone is engaging in the behavior, as well as the specific skills that need to be taught. This information will be used during treatment planning. Again, you can activate a screen share function or open a shared online document so that all participants can see a written summary statement while the content is being discussed. The summary statement can be used to check in with the consultees to ensure that all people agree with the target behavior and function of the behavior.

Design Intervention Plan

The next step within the PAI is to develop an intervention plan that will (a) reduce the likelihood that the behavior of concern will occur in the future and (b) increase the likelihood that the student will engage in a functionally equivalent replacement behavior. This will be done through a combination of antecedent manipulations (i.e., changes in the environment) and teaching specific skills. During this plan development, you will discuss relevant treatment components and inquire about the cultural fit within the school environment. This is an important step to maintain a good working alliance between you and the consultee. You are supporting remotely, so the consultee will be the direct implementor; thus buy-in is critical so that the consultee will change their own behavior.

After developing the intervention strategies, or relevant components, the treatment team will create a plan for how to go about implementing those strategies. This includes developing a training plan and allocating resources appropriately to ensure that the intervention will be implemented with high fidelity. If the consultee needs additional training, you should schedule additional meetings with the consultee to train them on the implementation strategies.

Throughout the PAI, you should check in frequently with the consultee regarding contextual fit and social acceptability of the procedures. At this stage, once an intervention plan has been developed, you can informally ask about the acceptability of the intervention. Alternatively, you can develop an online survey to assess for the intervention acceptability and send that link to the consultee, following the PAI meeting. Further details regarding specific plan design elements are discussed in Chapter 6.

Ongoing Data Collection and Meeting Summary

The final stage of the PAI is to develop a measurement plan for assessing the effectiveness of the intervention. In many cases, the data collected following the PAI may be sufficient to continue during intervention implementation. Additionally, the treatment team should develop a treatment fidelity tool that is feasible to collect data on, and accurately measure, implementation of the intervention (Sanetti & Collier-Meek, 2019). Finally, you will summarize what was discussed and schedule the next meeting. The next meeting may be for classroom observation, training, or further discussion of next steps.

AFTER CONDUCTING THE PAI

After the conclusion of the PAI through teleconsultation, you should briefly document the session in your session notes. Then, it is important to send a written summary of the meeting to the participants; this would include the summary statement and intervention plan. In some cases, this could be an FBA and behavior intervention plan report. In this email follow-up, clearly identify any action items for the consultees. Bolded text or a separate list within the email will help draw the recipient's attention to the key next steps. For this stage of teleconsultation, the action items may include further data collection, scheduling of training, or implementation of specific strategies in the classroom.

PROBLEM SOLVING DURING THE PROBLEM ANALYSIS STAGE

Some unique challenges can arise during the problem analysis stage. The biggest challenge is whether there are unclear contradictory outcomes from the data collected following problem identification. Additionally, the consultees, families, and related service providers may disagree regarding the outcomes of the data analysis or conceptual fit of the intervention. Further discussion is warranted in these situations. You should use what was learned from the rapport building in order to ensure that an effective working relationship is still in order (see Chapter 3 for further details).

Habituation to the Technology

The consultee may report that the analysis of the data collected is unexpected or is contrary to the typical presentation of data. Commonly during teleconsultation, you will use videoconferencing to observe the target student(s) and the consultee as a part of the data collection procedures. The presence of a computer device and observer may result in changes in observed behavior from both the teacher and students. If this is believed to be the case, you may turn off the camera/screen during observations or increase the frequency and duration of observations. When turning off their camera, you will still be able to observe the classroom, while the classroom will not be able to see that there is someone currently observing. This may help reduce student reactivity to observations. The teacher, however, may continue to change their behavior, as they will still be aware of the observations. Another possible solution is to persist with observations: An additional series of observations should help the teachers and students in the classroom habituate to observers in the room. Across time, their observed behavior may return to the baseline levels of behavior.

An additional consideration is if the pattern of observed behavior is different from what the consultee expected, you can explore other changes to the environment that might better explain the behavior change. As a result, you may recommend a change in referral or a termination of teleconsultation services.

Experimental Functional Analysis of the Problem

There are times when the information gathered during the problem identification stage is insufficient or inconclusive. The consultant can then continue to gather information. Alternatively, they may wish to conduct a functional analysis to experimentally determine the maintaining function of the target behavior. During a functional analysis, the consultant is manipulating the antecedents and consequences to experimentally assess under what contingencies the behavior of concern is most likely to occur. This is useful when the student is an individual student referral; other forms of additional data collection are better suited to classwide or schoolwide referrals. While the consultee conducts this in person with the student, the consultant can either be in person or supporting the process over videoconferencing. The consultant will first review the procedures to conduct a functional analysis over teleconsultation with the consultee, then they discuss conditions in which the consultant should conduct this assessment in person with the consultee and student. This is a procedure in which you need previous expertise and training prior to conducting over teleconsultation. If you do not have the expertise in conducting functional analyses, seek out supervision or a qualified service provider.

Functional analyses have been conducted over telehealth platforms with high fidelity and have resulted in clear differentiation of behavior (e.g., Barretto et al., 2006; Bloomfield et al., 2020; Machalicek et al., 2009). In these cases, the expert in functional assessment was remotely coaching a local provider, over videoconferencing, to implement the procedures. This is a useful procedure, as the experimental assessment can verify the functional hypotheses developed during the problem analysis stage. When conducted over teleconsultation, you use preimplementation training, bug-in-the-ear coaching, and video recordings to train the consultee, provide in-the-moment feedback, and record a permanent record for data analysis, respectively.

Once the team has decided that a functional analysis will be useful in providing a clearer pattern of behavior, you will then obtain consent from the student and their family. During the functional analysis, the behavior of concern will intentionally be evoked to observe under which contingencies the behavior is most likely to occur. Thus, explicit consent and clear safety precautions are needed before any procedures are to be conducted. If there are concerns for safety, or the target behavior is complex in nature, you may then need to use further indirect assessments or travel to the school for in-person assessment.

Following consent, you will train the consultee on the functional analysis procedures. This can take the form of behavioral skills training, where the consultant will remotely describe the assessment procedures, model the implementation of all steps of the functional analysis, and have the consultee engage in rehearsal of the conditions. This training can use asynchronous training modalities such as prerecorded webinars, reading materials, video examples, and the submission of video rehearsal with a confederate. The teleconsultant may also use synchronous training features, such as a live rehearsal with immediate performance feedback to the consultee. During all of these training procedures, the target student would not be in attendance.

For the implementation of the experimental functional analysis, the following materials are needed at the school:

- webcam for observation
- headphones for discreet feedback
- reliable internet connection
- protective equipment, if warranted
- academic or task demand materials (for a demand condition)
- preferred toys/tangible items (for a tangible condition)

The specific materials needed for the sessions, such as the academic demand materials and preferred tangible items, will be unique to the specific student and context for the functional analysis. These materials will be selected beforehand using information gathered by the teleconsultant during the problem analysis. The functional analysis conditions should most closely approximate the context in which the target behavior is likely to occur. Thus, the specific materials will vary for each student.

During the functional analysis procedure, you will first ensure that the camera is set up so that you have a good viewing angle of the room; you want to be able to view all instances of the target behavior from this vantage point. Then, you will turn off your camera. As best as is feasible, you want to make your observation of the student as discreet as possible so that the observed behavior approximates the typical context. You will communicate to the consultee through headphones in order to provide instructions and feedback without alerting the student. In this case, the consultee should use wireless Bluetooth headphones or a headset connected to a mobile device that can be stored in their pocket. When wireless headphones are not available, you can use a phone call with wired headphones for audio transmission.

To account for any possible delays in the audio/video feeds, the video feed microphone should be used while the phone microphone is muted. That way, the incoming audio is synchronized with the video of the student's behavior. Your microphone can then transmit in-the-moment feedback to the consultee's phone, where minor delays will not interfere with data collection.

Through the headphones, you will (a) direct the consultee regarding the procedures and (b) collect primary data for the functional analysis. For further data analysis, you should record the functional analysis; this can then be used to code secondary variables or complete interobserver agreement.

SOCIAL VALIDITY DURING THE PROBLEM ANALYSIS STAGE

Throughout this process, you should check in frequently with the consultee and other partners regarding the acceptability of the procedures. Using informal conversation and structured questionnaires, you can assess the consultee's experience with analyzing the problem. Other ways to assess social validity include gathering information on the consultee's comfort with implementing the procedures in their classroom, their agreement with the assessment and intervention plan developed, and their responsiveness to communication.

Also, if a teleconsultant incorporates the experimental functional analysis procedure, they should be prepared to discuss and demystify the process and clearly articulate why this form of FBA can clarify and support the behavior of concern. Because this FBA procedure inherently evokes the behavior of concern, there are social validity issues to consider before conducting it. Also, only individuals competent to conduct experimental functional analysis should do so, and during teleconsultation, the teleconsultant should have experience conducting experimental functional analysis procedures in person and through telehealth.

Further, teleconsultants who want to conduct an experimental functional analysis but experience apprehension from partners should refer to the article by Hanley (2012) that addresses the misunderstandings and practical obstacles behind functional analysis, in order to demystify the process for caregivers and educators. To increase social validity, Hanley suggested using open-ended interviews early in the formulation analysis and in subsequent procedures.

CASE STUDIES: PROBLEM ANALYSIS

Schoolwide Teleconsultation Referral

Zoe had been collecting data on her class's rate of academic engagement for the previous 2 weeks. Darian had been reviewing the data daily, updating the spreadsheet that he had created in their shared folder, and developing some preliminary hypotheses. Based on what he observed in the data, he saw that on average, about 50% of the class were engaged in Zoe's lessons but that there was a lower rate of engagement during the afternoons, which was when she did math instruction every day. He then scheduled a meeting with Zoe to review this information and conduct the PAI.

Darian began by thanking Zoe for her persistence in collecting data and for meeting with him during another one of her planning periods. Zoe was thankful that they were meeting to develop a plan; by collecting this information about her class, she was noticing how much the off-task behavior was impacting her class every day. Darian then shared his screen to show the data that had been collected. When Darian was summarizing these data, Zoe started to break down and cry. She felt that she was a bad teacher because her class wasn't paying attention while she was teaching. Darian paused the screen share and comforted Zoe; he assured her that it was clear that she cared about her students and was committed to making a difference in her classroom. He reminded her that they were collecting this information so that together, they could plan an intervention that would be effective and aligned with her classroom.

After reviewing the data and discussing what was most important for Zoe's classroom, Darian began to describe the preliminary ideas for intervention based on the data presented. First, he wanted to help Zoe and her class create their classroom expectations that would address these challenges that she had reported, and then they would implement an intervention. As the challenges in the classroom appeared to be across a group of students, he proposed a classwide intervention called "the good behavior game." This game was an intervention designed to reinforce appropriate classroom behavior by awarding points throughout the lesson. At the end of the game, the group of students with the most points would win and get to choose a prize from a list of options picked by the class. The game would be positively worded, focus on increasing more prosocial and academically engaged behaviors, and have students involved throughout.

Using the screen share function, Darian showed Zoe some example materials for the good behavior game and asked her what she thought of the intervention. Zoe started to smile, and she responded that she liked how positively focused the intervention would be. She said that because her class was respectful and got along nicely with one another, she thought the students would love the game and be eager to play.

The next steps would be for Darian to develop the intervention materials and train Zoe on the good behavior game. He said that all of the materials would be saved in their shared folder for her to access. He asked whether she had any questions about the intervention or their next steps. They then scheduled their next meeting and ended the teleconsultation session.

Intensive Needs Teleconsultation Referral

After about 2 weeks of data collection, which included a review of records and direct observations, Estella set up a problem analysis meeting with Wendy to discuss the data that they had collected after their PII and to work collaboratively in order to develop an evidence-based intervention that would support Nico's behavior at school. Once Wendy joined Estella, through videoconferencing, for the PAI, Estella began the meeting by thanking Wendy and her staff for their commitment to Nico and for all of their hard work collecting the ABC data and sharing records, as well as for allowing Estella to conduct digital observations of Nico. Then, Estella set the context for the problem analysis meeting by providing an overview of the day's discussion, and the goal of this stage of teleconsultation; they were seeking to understand why the behavior of concern was occurring and how they might approach an intervention to support Nico.

Estella shared her screen to show the data that she, Wendy, and Wendy's staff had collected across the previous 2 weeks. The results of the ABC data, direct observation, record reviews, and interviews showed that escape and attention functioned as rewards. As a result, they needed to understand the function of the behavior more comprehensively. In doing so, they would better understand the function of Nico's behavior and could develop a more individualized and effective intervention package.

As such, Wendy and Estella agreed to conduct an experimental functional analysis (FA) of the concerning behaviors in order to systematically understand the circumstances triggering and maintaining those behaviors. However, before beginning the planning for the FA, Estella and Wendy met virtually with Nico's parents in order to involve them in the planning process and to obtain additional and explicit consent for these additional behavior assessment procedures. There were various FA methods that Estella was competent in using, and she ultimately decided on an interview-informed brief functional analysis procedure (Coffey et al., 2020). They also wanted to use an FA procedure that was socially valid for the school environment— both from a training and an implementation standpoint. Wendy thought that the behavior of concern was likely maintained by access to adult attention and escape from challenging academic tasks, and, as such, they proposed conducting an FA. Estella spent time working with Wendy to understand what each of the conditions looked like during the school day—access to adult attention, escape from task, and play (i.e., the control condition)— and how they could replicate those conditions for Nico during the assessment. After Estella understood the conditions, she spent time developing materials to support training efforts with Wendy.

With the materials that Estella developed, she began a behavioral skills training approach to teach Wendy how to implement the FA conditions with Nico. Training started with an overview of FA conditions and procedures. After describing those procedures, Estella showed Wendy brief video clips of similar conditions that she had prepared for a previous case. While Wendy watched the video clip, Estella highlighted important procedural considerations. Wendy asked questions to clarify procedures, and Estella reviewed procedures for anything that was unclear. When Wendy felt confident with the procedures, Estella asked her whether she would be able to record a simulated session with one of the teacher support professionals in her class and send the recording to Estella to review and to provide feedback. After Wendy had done so and Estella had reviewed the simulated conditions, she met with Wendy to provide feedback and prepare for implementing the FA. Wendy affirmed that she was feeling confident to conduct the FA with Estella's support through videoconferencing and bug-in-the-ear training supports.

On the day of the FA, Wendy arranged for her other students to be elsewhere so that she and Nico could use the classroom context. Estella observed, collected data, and provided bug-in-the-ear feedback through videoconferencing.

Wendy was able to successfully implement the 5-minute conditions with minimal coaching and feedback, and Estella was able to collect useful data to better understand the behavior of concern. After two 1-hour assessment sessions, Estella thought that she had enough information to determine the function of the behavior of concern and use that information to develop function-based interventions. Figure 5.3 shows the per-minute rate of property destruction across sessions.

Estella noticed that compared with the control (play) condition, property destruction occurred during the escape and attention conditions, with higher rates of behavior during the escape condition. There was also much variability across sessions, and Wendy took the information considering the previous FBA context and corresponded with Wendy about the functions of the behavior of concern, which she determined was due to both escape from difficult instructions and access to adult attention. These findings confirmed initial hypotheses and helped ensure that interventions targeting both functions would be beneficial.

Wendy and Estella then met to discuss an individualized intervention that incorporated strategies to address both functions maintaining the behavior of concern. Wendy mentioned that in the past, she used a prevention strategy, noncontingent reinforcement, in which she proactively provided her attention to students whom she noticed needed more support and feedback. Estella really liked this strategy to help with the attention function they identified. Estella also mentioned that she would want to teach a new skill in place of

100 • *A Practical Guide to School Teleconsultation*

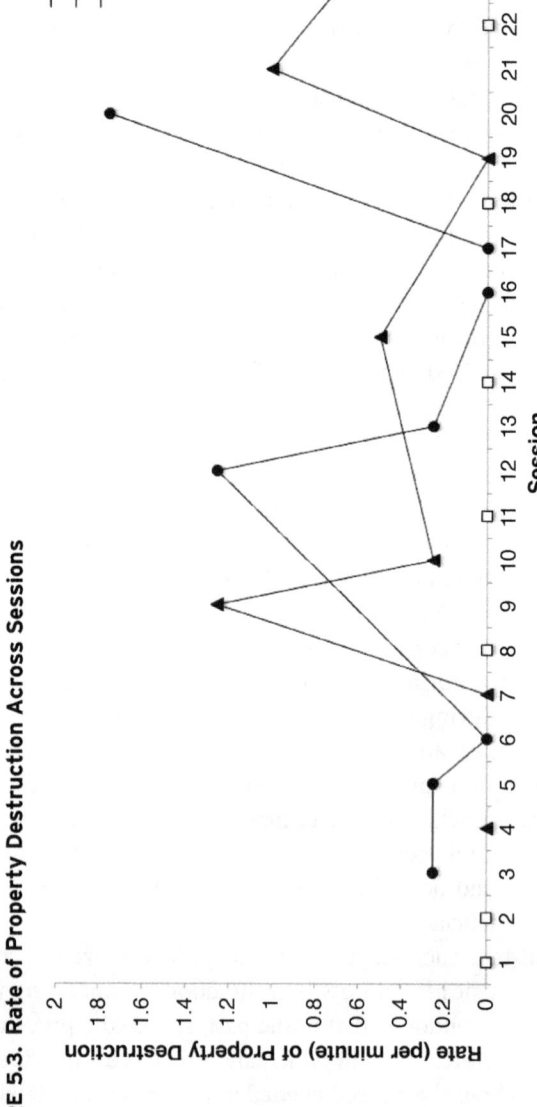

FIGURE 5.3. Rate of Property Destruction Across Sessions

property destruction. She proposed a functional communication training (FCT) intervention that would teach Nico how to request both adult attention or a break, dependent on which he desired in the moment (Tiger et al., 2008). Estella provided an overview of the FCT intervention, discussing previous students who used similar interventions and the success they observed. Wendy asked a few clarifying questions and explained how she thought that the interventions, both noncontingent reinforcement and FCT, would be great individualized strategies that she could use with her staff to support Nico.

Finally, Estella discussed with Wendy how to progress monitor Nico's behavior. Estella asked that Wendy record the times when Nico requests a break or attention and to note when he engages in the behavior of concern throughout the day. Wendy said that she would work with her classroom support staff to help, and Estella mentioned that she was available to help if needed. In the meantime, Estella drafted the behavior support plan and sent it to Wendy and to Nico's parents to review, provide feedback on, and consent to procedures.

6 INTERVENTION PLANNING, TRAINING, AND SUPPORT

Once you complete the post Problem Analysis Interview (PAI) activities, you are ready to prepare the intervention plan, provide training to consultees, and support ongoing implementation of interventions. In this stage, the consultee will implement the intervention and monitor the client's progress; you will virtually support the consultee through this process. It is important to note that the teleconsultant's role in this stage is to support learning and effective implementation of the intervention. Learning new content and applying those newly learned skills can be challenging for educators and staff, and teleconsultants should prioritize patient, compassionate, constructive, and responsive support. This chapter discusses the steps that teleconsultants should complete to support socially valid student outcomes—from intervention planning to supporting successful intervention implementation. We structure the intervention planning, training, and support from a behavioral approach; we are not discussing other models of service delivery. While this may be described as a time and resource process, it is similar for in-person service delivery. We discuss the best-practice guidelines for comprehensive intervention planning, training, and support; however, at the

---

https://doi.org/10.1037/0000366-006
Teleconsultation in Schools: A Guide to Collaborative Practice, by A. J. Fischer and B. S. Bloomfield
Copyright © 2024 by the American Psychological Association. All rights reserved.

end of the chapter, we discuss some modifications to the procedures to be feasible under various circumstances.

BEFORE INTERVENTION TRAINING SESSION

To best set up the consultee for success, you should proactively and intentionally plan for what will be required for the intervention. This will include student and consultee factors as well as relevant contextual variables necessary to promote successful implementation. This stage flows directly from the problem analysis stage where you were identifying the individual and contextual variables related to the target behavior. Through this functional behavior assessment process, the teleconsultation team has collaboratively identified a hypothesized function of the target behavior (or experimentally verified the function using functional analysis). You will use those data collected to inform intervention selection, develop all related materials, and gather input from all relevant parties.

Intervention Planning

The goal of intervention planning is to develop an ecologically valid, evidence-based intervention to address the goals of the consultee and student. To best do this, you are working collaboratively with the consultee to identify what is feasible, acceptable, and effective within the environment in which the consultee and student interact. As consultation is an indirect service model, the teleconsultant is often working with the consultee, who is supporting the student. It is important to include the student at the center of intervention planning. For a person-centered model of care, their interests, experiences, and goals must be prioritized when developing any support plan. This can include the student and their family participating in the discussion as well as trials of various strategies with the consultee and student. The first step in intervention planning is to identify strategies and interventions based on the identified behavioral function. Table 6.1 is a list of some suggested interventions and strategies, organized by behavioral function, for behaviors that are socially maintained.

An in-depth discussion of behavioral function and intervention strategies for nonsocially maintained behavior (sometimes called *sensory* or *automatic*) is outside the scope of this text. While in some cases, environmental strategies (e.g., antecedent interventions) can reduce the frequency or intensity of nonsocially maintained maladaptive behaviors, the assessment and intervention

TABLE 6.1. Strategies by Behavioral Function

Function	Strategies
Attention	• Positive adult attention (e.g., wandering the classroom randomly and increasing proximity to students who often engage in problem behavior) • Positive peer attention (e.g., peer tutoring) • Increased proximity to the student (e.g., moving the student's desk closer to the teacher's)
Escape	• Offering task choices (e.g., which task to complete, where the task can be completed) • Incorporating student interests into academic activities • Modification of task completion (e.g., using whiteboards rather than worksheets)
Tangible	• Mixing highly, moderately, and nonpreferred activities throughout the day in order to allow students opportunities to engage in preferred activities • Increasing accessibility to preferred item

process can be more complex; this may indicate an exclusively teleconsultation approach to be contraindicated. Please consult further resources for more direct guidance about the assessment and intervention of interfering behaviors that may be automatically maintained. For further information related to intervention identification, refer to related texts on school-based intervention selection, such as the following shown in Exhibit 6.1.

EXHIBIT 6.1. Suggested Texts for Behavior Supports in Schools

Collins, T. A., & Hawkins, R. O. (Eds.). (2021). *Peers as change agents: A guide to implementing peer-mediated interventions in schools*. Oxford University Press.

Hawken, L. S., Crone, D. A., Bundock, K., & Horner, R. H. (2020). *Responding to problem behavior in schools: The check-in, check-out intervention* (3rd ed.). Guilford Press.

Jimerson, S. R., Burns, M. K., & VanDerHeyden, A. M. (Eds.). (2016). *Handbook of response to intervention: The science and practice of multi-tiered systems of support* (2nd ed.). Springer. https://doi.org/10.1007/978-1-4899-7568-3

O'Neill, R. E., Albin, R. W., Storey, K., Horner, R. H., & Sprague, J. R. (2015). *Functional assessment and program development for problem behavior: A practical handbook* (3rd ed.). Cengage Learning.

Radley, K. C., & Dart, E. H. (Eds.). (2019). *Handbook of behavioral interventions in schools: Multi-tiered systems of support*. Oxford University Press.

Stormont, M. (Ed.). (2012). *Academic and behavior supports for at-risk students: Tier 2 interventions*. Guilford Press.

When identifying the intervention, you can test-drive different strategies with the consultee; you would demonstrate the intervention over videoconferencing, share a video example, or email a written description to them. They can then provide feedback on whether that intervention would be feasible for them or is something they could see within their classroom. To illustrate this process, teleconsultants should refer to Dart et al. (2012), a study in which the authors provided four educators with several intervention options and evaluated each in terms of their acceptability. They found that teachers implemented interventions with higher levels of integrity when they had the opportunity to select the intervention that they perceived as the most acceptable. The authors noted that test-driving interventions can bolster collaboration and treatment integrity, especially when consultees appear reluctant during the consultation process. It is important to get buy-in from all relevant partners prior to finalizing the intervention plan, as they will be the individuals responsible for the ongoing intervention implementation.

Some of this planning will have occurred during the PAI; however, there are times when additional planning meetings or communication is required to identify an intervention plan with the input of all team members. Once the team has agreed upon the strategies that are aligned with the implementation environment, you can finalize the written plan developed through the PAI. You should write a summary of the outcomes of the assessment procedures (e.g., outcome of PAI, functional behavior assessment report) and the corresponding intervention plan (sometimes called a behavior intervention plan or BIP). This intervention plan will describe the components of the intervention, the steps required for implementation, and who will be responsible for the implementation of the intervention. To help keep this easy for both the consultee and the teleconsultant, you can use the same data sheet from the behavior assessment procedures, as the target behavior and relevant outcomes are the same.

Additionally, you should write a training plan for the intervention. This is a step-by-step procedural guide for how you will be training the consultee on the intervention plan and how they will measure implementation fidelity. This written guide will be similar to the BIP previously developed yet will focus on the consultee skills. You will include an implementation fidelity checklist, which takes the form of a task analysis of the intervention implementation. For further information on the development and assessment of implementation fidelity, consult the Sanetti and Collier-Meek (2019) text titled *Supporting Successful Interventions in Schools: Tools to Plan, Evaluate, and Sustain Effective Implementation*.

Preparing Intervention Materials

Some of the interventions and strategies developed in the previous intervention and training plans will require materials or additional support for successful implementation. Prior to conducting the training with the consultee, you will develop and collate all relevant materials. You can create a digital shared folder of the resources for the consultee as well as prepare the physical content. For example, if the intervention uses a break card or point chart for an individual student, those materials might include language or images that are familiar to the student and aligned with their interests. In the development of materials for the student and the consultee, you should put effort into ensuring that the student, their language, and their culture are represented throughout. Using the information that you have previously gathered about the student, you can embed pictures of them or use their own words, in order to ensure that the materials are relevant and representative. Thus, you will likely be creating new materials for this student. Those materials may be digital, but you may also print, laminate, and gather all relevant materials to send a physical shipment to the consultee. Within this folder, you will add data sheets and the training guides, for easy access to the consultee.

Develop a Safety and Crisis Plan

You are responsible for supporting the safety of the student and the educators, and in some situations, the student you are supporting might engage in behaviors that become unsafe or reach a crisis level and subsequently require systematic supports. These behaviors can include harming oneself, harming others, or destruction of property. In the event that these are known to occur with the student, you and the consultee should develop a plan to be prepared for safety concerns around escalated and crisis behavior.

The safety and crisis plan should serve as a brief troubleshooting guide for the behavior support plan created through teleconsultation. The safety and crisis plan should be related to the intervention and describe who is responsible for different duties across different behaviors on the continuum of behavior ranging from stable and calm to being escalated or in crisis. The plan should specify whom to seek help from under different circumstances and include contact information for individuals or services available within the school, district, and community (e.g., mobile crisis outreach teams, stabilization, mobile response). When escalation or crises occur, it can be a stressful and unpredictable experience for all of the individuals involved. Because the teleconsultant cannot physically be in the space and, as such, cannot directly provide crisis intervention, they should set expectations about how they can support the consultee during those scenarios. For example, if you observe escalation or crisis during the videoconferencing session, you can be helpful by communicating with those predetermined individuals and thereby leaving the educator free to stay fully engaged with the situation at hand. We also discuss crisis response in Chapter 8, and the implications if these plans are not in place or accessible.

DURING INTERVENTION TRAINING SESSION

When you begin your training session with the consultee, you should orient them to the content of the session and explain the scope of the training. Use a systematic training methodology to ensure acquisition and mastery of the skill through telecoaching and telesupervision as suggested by Bloomfield et al. (2020). During teleconsultation, consultants should use behavioral skills training (BST; Kirkpatrick et al., 2019), which is a best-practice skill acquisition pedagogy. BST consists of consultant didactic instruction of the skill, consultant modeling of the skill, consultee rehearsal of the skill, and consultant performance feedback on the consultee's rehearsal. Researchers have demonstrated the effectiveness of BST in various staff training and support studies—a recent review by Kirkpatrick and colleagues (2019) showed that BST is an effective training modality for a variety of behavioral intervention procedures, including discrete trial teaching, incidental teaching, and the implementation of activity schedules.

The subsequent sections describe the BST model when applied to training educators and school staff on new skills that they can use in their classrooms and schools. (See also the Chapter 6 figures online at https://www.u-tteclab.com/book--text-resources.html.)

Discuss the Skill

The initial skill within the BST process involves the teleconsultant discussing the skills and interventions included in the plan they developed. This stage is didactic in nature, and you should begin by sharing your screen in order to present the written document of the intervention plan, as well as any slides that you may have developed for easily teaching the information. Consider this stage of the process as though you were conducting a webinar. Present the full content of the written document—but in a concise and engaging way. You should take time to go through each section, while providing ample opportunities to pause, check for understanding of the content, and allow consultees to ask questions about the steps, both conceptually and practically. It may be appropriate to include some questions to check for understanding with the skills and procedures described in this didactic session. There is emerging evidence that this stage can be completed asynchronously with prerecorded video or written instruction, which can be more time efficient if synchronous discussions are not feasible (e.g., Glover et al., 2019; Nese et al., 2020).

Model the Skill

After providing the initial didactic training on the intervention plan content, you should show the consultee how they should implement specific skills. This is a particularly important step that can be difficult to model through synchronous videoconferencing because of the image size available for consultees and the constraints of the content observed on screen. As such, we recommend that you use previously recorded video content through web-based resources or develop individualized video models for unique skills or scenarios. You can share your screen and use the video content to demonstrate how to implement the skills. Through this format, you can pause video, discuss questions or considerations with the consultee, and view the content as many times as needed in order to understand the nuance of implementation procedures. Alternatively, you can send these video files to the consultee to review on their own time.

In addition to prerecorded video models, you can use animated videos or scenarios to demonstrate the skill. We have found that the video animation software Vyond is very dynamic (i.e., easy to customize) and relatively easy for a new user to learn. With video animation, the video creator can design the scenario and adapt the included participants to the specific referral for a more nuanced and individualized demonstration. For example, the avatars can be adapted to look similar to the student and the consultee, and the background can be constructed to look like the environment that the consultee and student spend their time in at school. Some examples of these training videos are included through the Behavior Response Support Team program from the Granite School District and the University of Utah. These videos cover a variety of topics, are open source on the YouTube channel, and have been translated into seven languages for increased access to the content (https://www.youtube.com/c/behaviorresponsesupportteambrst). As in the previous step, you will follow up with the consultee regarding the modeling of the skill that occurred; you should check for understanding and answer any questions.

Rehearse the Skill

After the teleconsultant models the skill, the consultee practices it, in a simulated environment, with a peer educator or with the student. This stage of BST focuses on competency of the skill, and the consultee should be able to show you that they are able to effectively engage in the skill, in order to verify that they can implement it accurately. Depending on the skill and its implications or the intervention, you may recommend that the consultee rehearse the skill first, separate from the intended student. For example, if the consultee implements a behavior support plan with multiple intervention steps, you could break each skill down discretely and ask the consultee to simulate each step or conduct the steps incidentally while working with a student. The rehearsal stage of BST is an important opportunity for the consultee to receive initial performance feedback and meet a predetermined mastery criteria, or competency, before implementing the intervention with the student.

Provide Initial Performance Feedback

This initial performance feedback will be similar in practice to telesupervision or other training modalities conducted over videoconferencing. In telesupervision, the supervisor is providing training and feedback to their supervisee over technology. Here, there is a similar relationship in that the teleconsultant is observing and providing performance feedback to the consultee regarding the fidelity of their implementation of the intervention.

Oftentimes this initial performance feedback during the acquisition of the skill is conducted using role plays, or simulated opportunities for the consultee to demonstrate the skill. When possible, the consultee should simulate their skill performance with another person in an environment similar to the implementation setting. This may mean that they rehearse the skill in their classroom with another teacher or school staff member playing the role of the student. If that is not possible, you can take the role of the student, and the consultee can demonstrate the skill over videoconferencing. While this virtual demonstration is different from in-person implementation in practice, you may still be able to assess for fidelity to the intervention protocol.

Prior to moving from this rehearsal and performance feedback to implementing the intervention on an ongoing basis with the target student, you will assess intervention fidelity. The consultee must demonstrate fidelity prior to intervention implementation. This is the key aspect of the BST process; without performance feedback and measurement of implementation fidelity, the consultee does not get the chance to improve their skills. In other words, without receiving that feedback, they may not know if they are doing something incorrectly. This is a critical juncture in the process because you might have to suggest changes in the way that the consultee is implementing the intervention plan. There could be defensiveness or resistance when receiving this feedback. You can continue to use what they have learned through the rapport-building process to identify and assess how to maintain the therapeutic relationship and how to respond if there are ruptures in critical areas of the rapport.

There are multiple ways to provide performance feedback, just as there is more than one way to assess implementation fidelity. Throughout this text, we have discussed various ways to embed technology into your consultation practice. These include both synchronous and asynchronous means of communication, with a combination of audio, video, and textual information to be shared. For performance feedback, all of those variations can be included, as well, including text message, email, phone call, videoconference, and store-and-forward audio/video/textual information. These varied modalities can all be effective to deliver performance feedback. First, you can have a conversation with the consultee wherein you discuss the expectation for performance feedback. You can describe that you will be providing frequent guidance related to the intervention plan that you developed together. It is important for an observer to note information about the implementation fidelity in order to help have the best outcomes for the consultee and the student. During this conversation, they should discuss preferred modalities for feedback so that you can align your behavior to match the consultee. Table 6.2 provides the pros and cons of using the various technologies for feedback.

DURING THE INTERVENTION IMPLEMENTATION SESSION

In this stage, consultants can assist progress monitoring of student behaviors and the consultee's treatment integrity. *Treatment integrity* refers to the degree to which an intervention is delivered as intended (Gresham, 2009). One way of measuring adherence to an intervention is by calculating the percentage of steps correctly implemented. You first count the total number of steps included in the intervention. Then, you divide the number of steps implemented correctly by the total number steps and multiply by 100 (DiGennaro et al., 2007; Fiske, 2008). Consultants can create a treatment integrity data sheet that includes the sequential intervention components, checkboxes for each component, and the total percentage of integrity (using the above calculation). Each observation provides an overall percentage of treatment integrity, which you can use to monitor progress across sessions

TABLE 6.2. Ways to Provide Performance Feedback and Suggested Circumstances to Use the Performance Feedback Method

Modality of feedback	Considerations for feedback	
	Pros	Cons
Email	• Written record	• Delayed delivery and implementation
Text message	• Easy access and written record	• Boundaries of personal vs. work devices
Phone call	• Flexible—don't need to be around device with camera	• Hard to find time
Voicemail	• Flexible delivery time	• Unable to provide a visual guide with the feedback
Video model	• Permanent record of desired performance	• Requires greater time and resources to develop
Videoconferencing	• Live feedback	• Scheduling time can be a challenge • No physical prompting or on-site modeling available
Bug-in-the-ear	• Immediate audio feedback	• Requires detailed description and might not be effective for some complex behaviors • No physical prompting or on-site modeling available
In person	• Can include model, side-by-side implementation, and physical prompting	• Time/resource intensive
Store and forward	• Watch and provide written feedback or even record yourself giving the feedback	• Permanent product of observation exists—potential for privacy or security issues

and inform the evaluation of student outcomes. Similarly, you can create progress monitoring sheets for child behaviors based on the types (e.g., noncompliance) and dimensions (e.g., frequency, duration, intensity, latency) of behaviors.

This teleconsultation session should occur during the initial day the consultee implements the intervention. Unlike previously simulated implementation, which occurred during intervention training sessions, this session occurs in the authentic educational environment, with the student present in the educational space. You should make purposeful efforts to be available on the first day of intervention implementation, because a consultee's incorporating of a new procedure in the classroom or living space can be anxiety provoking, difficult, or frustrating, and you can mitigate some of those concerns as well as provide immediate performance feedback. One benefit of attending the initial intervention implementation session is the ability to be responsive; the teleconsultant can provide consultees support and in vivo performance feedback, especially if there is a high-intensity behavior or crisis.

When supporting your consultee on the initial day of implementation, be sure to set a positive and constructive atmosphere while you observe and leave the consultee with validation and affirmation of their efforts and relative successes. You should identify the consultee's preferred feedback method. Some examples of ways to provide feedback include delivering summative feedback at a designated time in the day through email or videoconference, providing immediate feedback through a text message, or arranging an alternative communication plan with the teacher.

AFTER THE TRAINING AND IMPLEMENTATION SESSIONS

After you conclude the observation of the consultee initially implementing the intervention, follow up with written correspondence. This communication should document the events that occurred during the implementation session and provide acknowledgment and encouragement to the consultee for their efforts implementing. Express gratitude to the consultee for allowing you to remotely join their classroom space to observe and reflect on the session with them.

PROBLEM SOLVING DURING THE PLAN IMPLEMENTATION

The following subsections describe ways that you can problem solve implementation issues at the various stages of BST—modeling, supporting implementation, and providing feedback.

Modeling the Skill

You may not have time to plan and record content to model skills to the consultee. In these scenarios, you can model the skill as you would in person, arranging your environment to adequately show elements of the intervention that you model for the consultee. You should find ways to use similar materials to what the consultee will use when implementing the intervention. You should browse the internet for asynchronous online resources (e.g., video examples, training materials), which have become increasingly available for a variety of interventions and skills since the beginning of the COVID-19 pandemic.

Supporting Consultee Implementation

When considering the training and implementation stage of problem-solving teleconsultation, screen for potential barriers that the consultee might experience before implementing the intervention. After the consultee implements the intervention, you should strive to continually assess their comfort with procedures, fidelity of implementation (discussed later in this chapter), and effectiveness for the socially valid student outcomes. This can be accomplished through ongoing discussions between the consultants and consultees and by directly observing the consultee's delivery of these supports via videoconferencing (Feldman & Kratochwill, 2003; H. C. King et al., 2022). Additionally, consider proactive inquiry through questionnaires that screen for potential issues. For example, the Parent Motivation Inventory (Nock & Photos, 2006) is a 25-item self-reported measure of parent motivation across three components, including (a) desire for child change, (b) readiness to change parenting behavior, and (c) perceived ability to change parenting behavior. Another example, the Barriers to Treatment Participation Scale (Kazdin et al., 1997), is a 44-item self-reported measure that assesses potential barriers to parents' treatment participation across four areas, including (a) stressors or obstacles that hinder treatment, (b) treatment demands, (c) perceived relevance of treatment, and (d) relationship with the therapist. Using one or both inventories can help you understand the context around the consultee's motivation for behavior change. As a note of caution, the contexts of both measures we described focus specifically on consultee caregivers and children, and teleconsultants who work with educators should adapt questions to reflect a consultee's context. After you understand the consultee's context, you can consider motivational interviewing strategies to address any ambivalence or resistance. During teleconsultation, you should be prepared to respond to and adapt to ambivalence or resistance, and when these instances arise, you should bring intentionality to rapport building to enhance motivation and subsequent implementation.

Providing Feedback

When synchronous observations are not viable, consultants should consider observing the sessions asynchronously through digital video and audio recordings. Upon obtaining the consultee's consent, and potentially the consent of other individuals (e.g., student's, classmates') who may be present in the videos, the consultant can ask the consultee to record the sessions and upload the videos to a secure, cloud-based storage platform (e.g., Google Workspace). Once the consultee successfully uploads the video, you can access it, open and position the electronic data collection sheet (e.g., target behavior, treatment integrity) beside the video display, press play, and proceed with data collection. Of note, various factors may impact the feasibility of obtaining the consent of all classmates (e.g., large classroom size, permission from classmates' caregivers, school district policy). Consultants and consultees could engage with school and district personnel to gauge the feasibility of obtaining the classmates' consent as needed. We discuss other applications of asynchronous teleconsultation in Chapter 9.

SOCIAL VALIDITY DURING PLAN IMPLEMENTATION

During the training and implementation stage of teleconsultation, every attempt should be made to create an environment that is collaborative and supportive—the context must resonate with the consultee. Especially at this stage, you should remind the consultee that everyone is learning—the student, the consultee, and the consultant—and that you will all get through this experience gleaning new information about the process and outcomes. Taking a person-centered, supportive, and culturally responsive approach to learning and pedagogy will help serve as a beacon to align your support efforts. This will help center the student's voice throughout the intervention process and support both the consultant and consultee in ensuring that the intervention plan is relevant and acceptable to the student and their family.

You should consider test-driving interventions with the consultee in order to allow the consultee and the student a choice in the strategies you ultimately choose to implement and maintain with the student (Dart et al., 2012). The consultee's perceptions of the effectiveness and acceptability of the intervention are other important aspects that you should consider, along with the student's perceptions. You should use a variety of measures to inform social validity and acceptability, including open-ended questions and measures. One measure related to intervention acceptability is the Intervention Rating Profile (IRP; Martens et al., 1985), which consists of 15 items rated on a 6-point Likert-type scale ranging from 1 (*strongly disagree*) to 6 (*strongly agree*) and includes questions assessing perceptions about whether an intervention is appropriate, effective, warranted, reasonable, and fair.

Positive engagement between families and educators is in the best interest of the student, school, and community. There are many obstacles to establishing and maintaining this relationship, but technological advances in recent years have allowed us to overcome these challenges and secure positive outcomes for the target student (Fischer & Bloomfield, 2020). School teleconsultants can invite both families and educators to participate in meetings, facilitate rapport-building activities with each other, and discuss each step of the problem-solving process with all members of the team in order to promote ongoing positive communication.

CASE STUDIES: INTERVENTION PLANNING, TRAINING, AND SUPPORT

Schoolwide Teleconsultation Referral

Prior to the training meeting, Darian sent Zoe a copy of the intervention materials through district mail and then emailed her a copy of the treatment integrity checklist. Darian then began the training meeting by reviewing all of the materials with her. He provided a description of what the good behavior game was, what the materials were to be used for, and why this was all relevant for her classroom. He then paused to answer any questions that she had.

Following the description of the intervention and written materials, Darian provided a model of the good behavior game. While he was talking with Zoe over teleconsultation, he shared a video example from a previous implementation. While playing the video, he talked over it, describing the key intervention components. Zoe then had some questions about how this intervention would work for her class. At this point, Darian broke down the intervention steps, referring to the treatment integrity checklist. While discussing the specific intervention steps, Zoe and Darian collaboratively identified some ways to make the intervention fit her classroom environment. She took some notes throughout.

Darian then asked Zoe to model the introduction of the intervention with him as though he was her class. She stood up, walked to the front of the classroom, and rehearsed the introduction of the good behavior game. Darian gave some performance feedback throughout the rehearsal, where he described elements that she had implemented with high fidelity, and other changes that she could make in order to improve her implementation. They rehearsed this some more until Zoe was demonstrating high fidelity and until she felt confident that she was ready to implement the good behavior game with her class. Darian then ended the teleconference session with a plan of when he would observe her implementation and how she could get some additional support if needed.

One week later, Darian called into Zoe's classroom to observe her implementation of the good behavior game. Zoe was demonstrating high fidelity with introducing the rules of the game, but once she went back to her teaching, she was observed to frequently stop her teaching in order to reprimand students for disruptive behavior. Because she was not engaging in high rates of praise to students displaying appropriate classroom behavior, she was not providing many points to the teams who were engaging in the desired behavior. While her fidelity was overall moderate, Darian would have liked Zoe to engage in more behavior-specific praise during her lesson and correspondingly award more points for good behavior during it. Darian and Zoe discussed this in a separate phone call after the lesson, when the class had gone outside for recess. Darian then proposed that his next recommendation would be for Zoe to receive some in-the-moment coaching from him over teleconsultation; he would provide feedback to her using bug-in-the-ear technology, where Zoe would be wearing one wireless headphone while teaching.

During the next class day, Zoe received in-the-moment feedback from Darian, and she noticed that the class was responding to the higher rates of praise that she was delivering during her lesson. She needed some prompts to ignore the disruptive behavior—but overall, her class was more engaged. Darian observed again the following day, without the performance feedback, and noticed that Zoe was implementing the good behavior game with high fidelity. He then continued to observe her implementation for a few more weeks.

Intensive Needs Teleconsultation Referral

After completing the experimental functional analysis on the behavior of concern and determining the function of the behavior, Estella designed a function-based intervention that Wendy and her staff would implement with Nico. Estella spent time writing up a functional behavior assessment that informed a function-based behavior support plan. She sent this plan to Wendy, and Wendy previewed the content prior to their next meeting. At the plan implementation meeting, Wendy and Estella discussed the plan and reviewed how to implement the intervention components. Similar to the training provided for the experimental functional analysis of the behavior of concern, Estella also provided a BST approach to supporting Wendy.

After discussing the intervention components, Estella played prepared video clips showing her effectively using the skill with a different student, whom she supported in person. Wendy and Estella watched the video clips together and continued the conversation around some of the nuances of functional communication supports. After watching the video model, Wendy practiced the intervention steps with one of her classroom support staff, and Estella observed while writing notes about the rehearsed implementation. Once Wendy and her colleague completed the rehearsal, Estella provided an affirmation for Wendy's efforts and for practicing the skill. Also, Estella showed appreciation for Wendy engaging in steps toward high-quality implementation. After verifying Wendy's competency to implement the functional communication procedures, Estella decided on a time that Wendy would begin the intervention with Nico and planned to attend and provide remote feedback and support. Before wrapping up the intervention training session, Estella reviewed the data collection procedures that they would use to progress monitor functional communication, along with the behavior of concern, for which they had ongoing progress-monitoring data.

On the day of implementation, Estella prepared to support Wendy and Nico by setting up the digital data collection system and joined the meeting at the designated time. Estella checked in with Wendy when she signed in to the videoconference, specifically to make sure that Wendy was feeling confident about implementing the intervention and to see whether she had any lingering questions. Wendy told Estella that she was ready to implement the intervention and was feeling comfortable with Estella providing feedback. During implementation, Wendy conducted the intervention procedures extremely well, with adherence to most of the steps outlined in the functional communication training procedure. Because the procedures initially called for teaching Nico to reliably request help, Wendy spent the first intervention session teaching him to request help by raising his hand and saying, "This is hard. I need help, please." Wendy presented Nico with difficult assignments, and following each time she read him the instructions, he asked for help but still broke the pencil he was using. Although there was an initial increase in Nico's functional communication response, the intervention did not necessarily reduce some of the mild property destruction previously observed. Estella thought that this could be due to Nico's learning history related to this behavior and had an idea to help reduce the behavior of concern, along with maintaining the increased functional communication. Through a bug-in-the-ear device, Wendy heard Estella ask her to present Nico with a new pencil but to mention that if he could keep his pencil safe while they were working together, he could earn some special time to play a game together. Nico excitedly agreed and took the new pencil, eager to continue with work. Wendy presented the instructions again, and this time, Nico asked for help and kept his pencil "safe." Wendy looked at the camera, smiled at Estella (who had her screen off), and mouthed "Thank you!"

At the end of the session, Wendy played a game with Nico, and afterward, a classroom support staff member took him to a group activity with his peers. Estella turned her camera on and praised Wendy for her tremendous effort and responsiveness with suggestions and feedback. Wendy mentioned that she thought that the intervention had worked well and was happy to see Nico's responsiveness. She mentioned also that she and her staff were trying to be more intentional about providing frequent noncontingent praise to Nico throughout the day. Wendy left the meeting feeling confident to implement the procedures in the classroom setting and collect ongoing data. Estella planned for a follow-up observation later in the week and graphed data and sent an email to summarize the observation and first day of implementation.

7 EVALUATION OF THE SCHOOL TELECONSULTATION PROCESS AND OUTCOMES

During the final stage of teleconsultation, the teleconsultant, consultee, student, and other partners evaluate the effectiveness of the designed plan. Additionally, you will assess for consultee and student acceptability. The purpose of evaluation at this stage is to guide the team through understanding whether the teleconsultation goals have been met—and, if so, plan for the discontinuation of teleconsultation services. If the goals have not been met, you are supporting the team with identifying relevant modifications necessary for continuation of services. This chapter guides you through the processes to evaluate the effectiveness and acceptability of teleconsultation. While this is not a comprehensive guide to evaluation procedures, the following sections highlight the ways in which you can apply technology to your evaluation process.

BEFORE THE PLAN EVALUATION SESSION

During this stage, we are collating data and looking at it in an aggregate fashion through graphs and meetings to discuss trends and changes in patterns of behavior. As we evaluate the information available, it is important to

---

https://doi.org/10.1037/0000366-007
Teleconsultation in Schools: A Guide to Collaborative Practice, by A. J. Fischer and B. S. Bloomfield
Copyright © 2024 by the American Psychological Association. All rights reserved.

understand the extent to which the intervention was implemented as planned (i.e., treatment integrity) and the extent to which the intervention positively impacts student outcomes. Before meeting with the consultee, you will develop a variety of visual guides to represent the data that were collected. Graphs and tables are two ways to represent data in a visual way for readers (Zoder-Martell et al., 2013). Any graphs that teleconsultants create should be designed in a clear and representative way, so that the consultee(s) and student(s) are able to easily infer information. Radley and Dart (2019) provided excellent parameters for scaling and designing visual analysis graphs for convenient and reliable interpretation of the data.

There are a variety of existing measures and procedures that you can consider when looking to assess the outcomes of the consultation process, and you should look beyond simply intervention effectiveness. There are other relevant outcomes that will impact the consultee and student that should be considered, such as the acceptability of the intervention, the use of technology, and the process of consultation. Further, you can assess the staff member's perceived effectiveness of the intervention. Similarly, an assessment of the consultee's *self-efficacy*—or their belief in their ability to implement the intervention—is useful in order to assess whether they may be ready to proceed without your services. Other related outcomes, such as the stress and well-being of the students, parents, and staff, are also critical for assessing the impact of the teleconsultation program.

Before the meeting, you should prepare information related to the social validity of the intervention. Separately, you can assess the social validity of both the technology platform and the consultative process (see Table 7.1 for

TABLE 7.1. Example Measures for the Assessment of Social Validity

Domain	Measures	Author(s)
Intervention acceptability	Behavior Intervention Rating Scale	Elliott & Treuting, 1991
	Intervention Rating Profile	Witt & Elliott, 1985
Technology acceptability	Technology Acceptance Model-Fast Form	Chin et al., 2008
Consultation process	Consultant Evaluation Form	Erchul, 1987
Staff well-being	Parenting Stress Index	Abidin, 1997
	Index of Teaching Stress	Greene et al., 1997
	Professional Quality of Life Scale	Stamm, 2009
	Maslach Burnout Inventory	Maslach & Jackson, 1981
	Teacher Subjective Wellbeing Questionnaire	Renshaw et al., 2015

example measures). Some of these data have been collected throughout the consultative relationship; however, this is the time to deliver a formal measure of acceptability following implementation. You can use a variety of online survey platforms to achieve this goal; these platforms support the collection, analysis, and presentation of social validity data between the teleconsultant and consultee. Upon gathering all of that information and compiling visual representations of it all, the teleconsultant, the consultee, and related partners can meet and discuss the evaluation of the intervention program.

DURING THE PLAN EVALUATION SESSION

At this meeting, all included members of the assessment and intervention will discuss the effectiveness of the teleconsultation process thus far. The goal of the meeting is to identify the next steps for supporting the consultee and student with the initial referral goal. While it may not be appropriate to have the student at the meeting when discussing the implementation fidelity of the consultees, it is relevant to ensure that the discussion centers the student. The student may be better situated to be included in other aspects of the plan evaluation, such as discussing goal attainment and any future goals. This is similar to the initial meetings, when the student voice is included in setting the goal and developing the intervention supports.

You have already gathered, compiled, and prepared all of the data for visual display to the team. At this point during teleconsultation, ideally, the rapport between the teleconsultant and consultee is well established; it should be a familiar and comfortable interaction between all individuals. Using the work completed throughout the previous stages, the consultant will review progress thus far and discuss next steps through videoconferencing. It is important that the relationship is strong at this point because part of the feedback that you would provide as a consultant has to do with the proficiency of the consultee to implement the intervention as planned.

To begin the plan evaluation meeting, welcome all attendees and introduce the purpose of the day's session. This includes deciding whether the student has met their goals and whether it is time to terminate teleconsultation services. You may then begin the discussion by sharing your screen on the videoconferencing platform and displaying the graphic representation of the intervention data. You should orient the observers to the graphs and vocally describe the results displayed on the screen. In addition to presenting the student behavior, you may display the treatment fidelity data to the team, demonstrating the level to which the consultee implemented the intervention as planned. It is important to celebrate the progress of the consultee and student throughout, using behavior-specific praise (Ennis et al., 2020). For example, you might say to the consultee,

> You've done a great job praising the student's use of the break card to request a break when needed. We are starting to see a change in his behavior in class. Keep up the great work, and we should continue to see more progress!

Upon reviewing the data and feedback with the team, you will support the team in making decisions about what is next. Asynchronous interactions (e.g., email, text) can be used to supplement the synchronous interactions as needed, especially when there is a time constraint for either or both parties. Regarding insufficient progress toward consultation goals, as evaluated through direct observation and collected data, the consultation team should consider reassessing the problem and target goals and modifying intervention plans when needed. We discuss further application of asynchronous teleconsultation in Chapter 9. We also provide a decision tree that you can use to help navigate practical scenarios. This model is described in the next section.

Teleconsultation Goal Met

If the teleconsultation goal has been met, the team should review the intervention fidelity data. When the goal has been reached and fidelity has been achieved, you can assist with the fading of support for both the student and consultee. After affirming that there has been adequate fidelity, the team should begin to plan for maintenance and generalization of the intervention for the student. Regarding the consultee, the team will develop a plan to fade out support, contingent on ongoing success.

If the goal has been met, yet the intervention was not implemented with fidelity, additional variables might better explain the change in the student behavior. You can assess other environmental variables that might better explain the behavior change. For example, if the student started some medication and the teleconsultation team was unaware, that might explain some of the behavior change that was observed. In relation to the consultee behavior, the teleconsultation team should review the fidelity data in more detail. The behavior change might be explained by the consultee implementing the core, or active, ingredients of the intervention. To better assess why that may be the case, the treatment team can analyze the fidelity data by each component or conduct a component analysis.

Teleconsultation Goal Not Met

Similar to when the goal has been met, when your goal has not been achieved yet, it is important to consider both consultee and student variables. If the intervention was implemented with fidelity, the team should review the previously collected problem analysis interview data. There may be some missing information that was not collected during the first assessment. If the intervention is implemented with fidelity yet there has not been a corresponding change in the student's behavior, the intervention may not be appropriately addressing the function of the target behavior. Additionally, there may be unmeasured implementation variables that are impacting the effectiveness of the intervention as designed. The team may return to that teleconsultation stage to collect further data and plan for a new intervention.

If the goal has not been met and the intervention was not implemented with high fidelity, you can proceed with a few additional steps with the consultee. You can continue providing coaching with the consultee in order to increase their implementation fidelity. This can be conducted remotely during separate sessions, remotely yet live during implementation (e.g., bug-in-the-ear coaching), or live and in person. You can assess whether it is feasible or necessary to shift to in-person coaching in order to increase implementation fidelity. Through this process, you are assessing your working alliance with the consultee—a rupture or poor working relationship between the teleconsultant and consultee may result in inconsistent implementation fidelity. If this is a concern, please revisit the rapport-building strategies discussed in Chapter 3. Finally, you should discuss the social validity of the intervention. Lower acceptability of the intervention is related to lower fidelity of implementation.

AFTER THE PLAN EVALUATION SESSION

Once you conduct the plan evaluation session, you should send an email to the consultee(s) and follow up—documenting action items and anything salient that should be recorded or referenced from the meeting. Then, depending on the outcome of the plan evaluation session, you should follow through with the next steps that you identified with the consultee. The content below describes various decision points and the respective teleconsultation responsibilities associated with each.

Continue the Intervention With Ongoing Coaching and Performance Feedback

When you find that the consultee needs initial support with implementing the intervention, you should discuss the opportunity to remotely observe once per week and support any concerns and answer questions. During these weekly meetings, you can also provide ongoing feedback about intervention implementation and help problem solve any new concerns or barriers that arise. Teleconsultants who provide ongoing performance feedback and coaching should work to maintain strong rapport with their consultee through engagement and the presence-building activities discussed in Chapter 3. Additionally, you should work to empower the consultee with the necessary skills and to fade your support, to the extent possible.

Reassess the Student's Context

You might find that the consultee is implementing the intervention procedures as planned but that the student outcomes measured don't show improvements. In this circumstance, return to the problem-analysis stage in order to more deeply understand the context. You should collaborate with educators and caregivers to collect more or different data to inform the behavior of concern. In your initial analysis, did you miss some context that changes your understanding of the behavior of concern? More information about the context, across settings, will help you to understand the reason(s) why the behavior is occurring and to select an intervention that could account for the student's circumstances in the various contexts. This outcome might also highlight that the intervention plan itself was not centering the student throughout the process; revisit the problem identification and analysis with an increased focus on the student's goals, interests, and preferences. Through assessing the student's voice, the consultant may identify that there is a rupture in the relationship between the student and the consultee that is impacting the student's progress.

Continue the Intervention and Layer in Another Component of a Multicomponent Plan

With data guiding the process, and with additional information you gleaned from reassessing the student's context, you can help consultees enhance gains or reductions further than current levels. Some aspects you might want to enhance include larger magnitude improvements, higher frequency engagement, and increased duration of target skills and behaviors. In those scenarios, you should work collaboratively with the consultee(s) to layer in additional supports, while following the procedures for intervention training described in Chapter 6. As we mentioned at the beginning of this section, the ongoing progress-monitoring data collected during the intervention evaluation stage will help you to understand the additive efficacy of intervention that you decide to layer into the behavior support plan.

Maintaining Services With Less Frequent Consultation

As the intervention and fidelity data show stability at the desired levels, you can fade how often you connect with the consultee. You can continue to monitor progress through electronic data collection systems; however, meetings to discuss data and provide feedback to consultees should occur less frequently if this path is selected. Building and empowering independent implementation of the skills is the teleconsultant's goal, and having the consultee maintain their skills with limited or no support builds the educator's or caregiver's capacity to implement similar interventions in the future.

Following Up After Some Time

In Chapter 3, we discussed the importance of following up with your consultee to build and maintain rapport. Similarly, during the plan evaluation stage, if your consultee is able to implement the procedures with fidelity, you should afford them the chance to implement the procedures with more independence—however, follow up with them to ensure that additional support is available, if needed. Monthly or quarterly follow-up meetings with your consultee can be helpful, as those meetings give you (a) an opportunity to provide responsive services (e.g., if student outcomes regress) or (b) a chance to maintain the rapport with the consultee, if you collaborate with them in the future. We recommend that you schedule follow-up emails to check in with consultees and make every attempt to differentiate the amount of follow-up, depending on the level of need. For consultees who are continuously implementing interventions well and do not require frequent teleconsultant support, periodically sending positive follow-up emails that acknowledge the consultees' sustained implementation efforts can be beneficial.

PROBLEM SOLVING DURING THE PROBLEM EVALUATION STAGE

Similar to problem solving during the other teleconsultation stages, during the evaluation stage, you will need to consider conceptual and practical issues that affect the consultation process. Particularly during the plan evaluation stage, you might have exhausted your ability to provide supports remotely, and there may be times when you need to attend locations in person. This is especially true if (a) the progress with implementation is insufficient; (b) despite attempts with adequate fidelity, you lack context to understand the behavior of concern; or (c) you need to provide on-site supports for recommendations that need intensive modeling, coaching, and performance feedback. In these cases, the service delivery model should shift from telehealth to in person, or you should refer to local providers.

SOCIAL VALIDITY DURING THE PROBLEM EVALUATION STAGE

It is also important to consistently measure the social validity of teleconsultation. Prior treatment acceptability and outcome research indicates that researchers (Ferguson et al., 2019; Wolf, 1978) tend to view social validity as two constructs: (a) the extent to which the consultee continues to deliver the intervention in the absence of their consultant (i.e., between teleconsultation meetings; Kennedy, 2002; Schwartz & Baer, 1991) and, more subjectively, (b) the consultee's and student's opinions about treatment goals, procedures, and the effectiveness of those procedures (Ferguson et al., 2019).

Ideally, as a teleconsultant, you effectively collaborate with the consultees and position yourself into a place where you need only to maintain and check in with the consultees, rather than have to provide ongoing and frequent levels of support across consultees. As caseloads increase, you need to differentiate how you provide consultees and students with ongoing support, especially once students and educators achieve the outcomes that teleconsultants and consultees initially aspired to improve. Assessing social validity in terms of a consultee's continued delivery of an intervention postconsultation (i.e., intervention maintenance) reflects the appropriateness of an intervention, based on the resources available and effort required of the consultee.

Social validity can also be indirectly assessed with questionnaires and rating scales. Considering teleconsultation's reliance on technology as a modality through which services are provided, it is important to capture whether the consultee perceived technology as an acceptable modality of service provision for behavior change. You should consider different social validity domains during teleconsultation (e.g., acceptability, feasibility, ease) and across different respondents (e.g., educators, students, caregivers). In addition to these social validity domains, you should also collect open-ended qualitative information that augments data from the quantitative measures.

CASE STUDIES: TELECONSULTATION EVALUATION

Schoolwide Teleconsultation Referral

After a few weeks of observing Zoe's implementation of the good behavior game, where Darian had limited performance feedback to provide, he scheduled a plan evaluation meeting with Zoe. At this meeting, Darian reviewed the changes in both her behavior and her class's academic engagement. When Zoe began to implement the intervention with high fidelity, her class increased their rate of academic engagement, and there were significantly fewer disruptions in the classroom. Zoe described how much more confident she was to manage her classroom and reported that she was now able to successfully complete her lessons with her class much more frequently. While some days were still more demanding than others, Zoe was experiencing success overall with her class—particularly during afternoon math lessons, which had been the most challenging before. Her class seemed to like the good behavior game, with them even asking about when they could play it again. Zoe did notice that there was still one student in her class, who engaged in the most talk-outs during lessons, for whom the prizes in the good behavior game did not seem to be significant motivators.

Darian's observations of the classroom supported Zoe's report. There was one student who was still having some difficulty with staying on task, but as this intervention had been successful for the majority of Zoe's class, she and Darian were happy with this progress; Darian was going to fade his support for the classwide intervention. Zoe and Darian discussed referring this student to the school's student-support team for a more individualized support plan. Darian mentioned that there were some Tier 2 interventions that could provide a little more specific supports for this student, and that was the next step to meet the needs of her class.

Intensive Needs Teleconsultation Referral

After completing the intervention training and implementation stage, Estella continued to support Wendy and Nico through ongoing classroom observations and communication, both through email and in passing, at the conclusion of each observation. Wendy also continued to record progress-monitoring data on the digital data collection tool that Estella created to support Nico. Additionally, during the observations, Estella gathered data on Wendy's fidelity implementing the intervention for Nico, and this afforded opportunities for Estella to provide ongoing performance feedback—although, after the initial intervention training session, Estella rarely needed to provide constructive feedback to Wendy, and the majority of the sessions were implemented without procedural concerns. The combination of Wendy's progress-monitoring data and Estella's digital observations provided context for the effectiveness of the intervention to improve Nico's functional communication in requesting help with challenging schoolwork, and a reduction in property destruction.

After collecting these data for 2 weeks and providing performance feedback, Estella connected with Wendy to set up the plan evaluation meeting and invited Nico's parents to join, as well. In this meeting, which all consultees attended, Estella discussed the observed reduction of Nico's property destruction, and the concurrent increase in his requesting help during difficult tasks. Nico's parents both expressed how happy they were and how they were also seeing Nico requesting help with difficult tasks at home rather than engaging in property destruction. Estella commented about how excited she was, not only for the supports impacting Nico positively at school but also that there was a collateral impact at home.

After reviewing Nico's progress, the teleconsultation team discussed how they could maintain and continue to generalize the skills in other settings, such as at Nico's family gatherings and elsewhere in the school. Nico's parents signed off the call, and Wendy stayed on the meeting to wrap up the conversation with Estella. Wendy mentioned how happy she was with the collaboration and the positive gains with Nico. She said that she planned to consider these interventions for other students in the future and would reach out to Estella for any support with difficult behaviors in her classroom down the line, especially if the behaviors necessitated a collaborative functional analysis. Estella told Wendy that she would be in touch in about a month, through email, to see how progress was going, to review data, and for support with anything that might come up between meetings.

PART III

BARRIERS TO SCHOOL TELECONSULTATION AND FUTURE DIRECTIONS

INTRODUCTION: BARRIERS TO SCHOOL TELECONSULTATION AND FUTURE DIRECTIONS

Although teleconsultation services are feasible and effective to support a variety of student concerns, individuals who are interested in conducting services through that modality should understand the benefits along with the limitations, as it relates to their practice. This is similar to the decision making used for in-person consultation and therapeutic service. You should be able to differentiate your service delivery to support a variety of students and consultees. This is applicable to all aspects of training, research, and practice. We need to train people how to engage in teleconsultation, further develop the research, and intentionally consider the practice so that the experience is optimal for the consultant, the consultee, and the student.

The chapters in Part III describe the barriers to teleconsultation and how you can navigate them in order to center the impact of the services on the student. Additionally, we provide a glimpse into what the future of teleconsultation looks like and encourage interested trainers, researchers, and practitioners to use teleconsultation with their teaching, research, and service, respectively.

8 NAVIGATING BARRIERS TO SCHOOL TELECONSULTATION

As does in-person consultation, practicing consultation through technology brings many potential barriers that consultants must consider. How teleconsultants plan for and navigate these inevitable barriers influences the overall process and outcomes. You should approach the teleconsultation process with a flexible perspective—one that invites a rich discourse with all partners—while understanding that behavior change is incremental and that thoughtful shaping procedures will likely be involved, especially for scenarios with more barriers present. You should assume that your consultees are approaching the consultation experience with positive intentionality and that they are engaging in the teleconsultation process to the best of their ability. Further, you should assume that your consultees are approaching the experience with a centering of the voices and needs of the students throughout the process.

You should work closely with your consultees to identify potential barriers to an equitable consultative experience. Consultants can use different methods to assess, plan for, and respond to barriers that may arise during teleconsultation. To the greatest extent possible, consultants should identify

https://doi.org/10.1037/0000366-008
Teleconsultation in Schools: A Guide to Collaborative Practice, by A. J. Fischer and B. S. Bloomfield
Copyright © 2024 by the American Psychological Association. All rights reserved.

potential barriers as early as possible and modify procedures accordingly prior to the delivery of teleconsultation. Teleconsultants should try their best to anticipate any barriers and respond promptly to barriers when they occur. Waiting a long period of time to address barriers (or not addressing them at all) creates space for ineffective communication and decreased consultee motivation and can contribute to consultee ambivalence and resentment toward the teleconsultation process. This is particularly important when considering your inability to provide hands-on support and be present compared to in-person consultation services. In this chapter, we describe teleconsultation barriers, including systemic concerns, technical and computing issues, difficulty planning and organizing for sessions, and preventing and responding to crisis or high-intensity concerns.

SYSTEMIC BARRIERS

Students who are marginalized within school communities experience many systemic barriers within the school system and within their community (Belser et al., 2016). When teleconsultants support students who experience these systemic issues, they should expect that a central part of the teleconsultation experience will be to promote educational equity by providing access not only to culturally responsive, evidence-based academic, social–emotional, behavioral, and mental health supports but also to computing technology and the internet. When these systemic barriers are intentionally addressed through policy and practice, you can provide supports and resources in ways that were previously limited due to geographical constraints. The subsequent sections of this chapter delve into some of the common systemic barriers that teleconsultants, consultees, and students might experience throughout the process and provide some suggestions for how to collaboratively address those barriers.

Access to Hardware and Software

Many schools furnish computing devices to students so that they can engage in virtual learning, allowing for equitable access to those devices and the needed software (e.g., Zoom, Microsoft Teams). Although many schools provide necessary technology to students and educators, this is not guaranteed across schools and districts, and there can be inequities in who accesses available technology. Confirming accessibility to current—and functioning—technology is important in order to successfully engage with the consultee or student. You may collaborate with the school and various external partners to furnish the required technology if the student does not have the prerequisite hardware. Alternatively, you may modify your procedures to work within the technological constraints currently in place, such as meeting in person when feasible and using more phone and email communication.

Internet Access and Speed

About 25% of Americans experience limited or impacted access to a home broadband connection due to socioeconomic constraints, and 15% of adults in the United States solely use a smartphone with internet access to fulfill their connectivity needs (Perrin, 2021). Although most schools in the United States have internet access, families may not have it in their home setting, which may create access barriers to collaboration. Despite the accessibility of hardware and software that schools provide, when students go home to do work, they will not necessarily have reliable access to the internet, let alone a stable, high-speed connection. Bandwidth fluctuations occur through any data service provider, and multiple individuals present within a student's learning space who also use the internet can limit the available bandwidth (i.e., slow the rate at which data is transferred across the internet). Bandwidth variability can result in video and audio lagging (e.g., becoming pixelated or choppy), cause dropped calls, or contribute otherwise to a poor teleconsultation experience. One videoconferencing provider, Zoom, suggests a minimum internet bandwidth speed of 2.0 Mbps (both for download and upload) in order to adequately engage in a one-to-one call; however, additional bandwidth is needed commensurate with the number of users on a call, especially for those who are using the screen share function. For example, if your internet connection in a living space is 25 Mbps, you will have adequate bandwidth for one user. However, if you have four to five users simultaneously engaging with content, especially video, you will likely have too slow of an internet connection and experience disruptions throughout the call.

Further, related to the systemic nature of broadband internet accessibility, recent research into digital and information redlining suggests that disproportionate access to information and inequitable broadband speed and access may be systemically restrictive toward individuals with lower income or who are Black, Indigenous, or people of color (Hall, 2021). One suggestion for supporting internet availability is to provide students and families with access to libraries, which provide communities free digital access and literacy programs. Alternatively, as suggested previously, phone and email communication are more accessible and require fewer resources than videoconferencing.

COMPUTING BARRIERS AND TECHNICAL BARRIERS

In addition to the systemic barriers that students and caregivers experience in their communities and schools, there are also computing barriers and technical barriers that pose unique challenges related to navigating the technology. The following sections describe both of these types of barriers that teleconsultants and consultees may experience, as well as some proposed ways to mitigate them.

Computing Barriers

Although teleconsultants and consultees will require the necessary computing technology to engage in teleconsultation, once they have access to the needed computing devices and software, they can still experience computing barriers. Individuals engaging in teleconsultation will likely have varying device age for their tablets, computers, and smartphones. Due to this factor, both you and your consultees will need to ensure that your devices' computing technology provides the minimum capabilities for effective teleconsultation practice—this includes frequently updating software. These extra steps to keep technology current and functional can be cumbersome; however, they are necessary in order to optimize the performance of the computing tools—and, ultimately, the teleconsultation services provided. When teleconsultants serve multiple consultees, it can be helpful to set up an organized system to track updates and verify that those updates are available across all devices that consultees use.

In addition to updating and maintaining computing hardware and software, when devices are in living spaces (rather than schools), other individuals in the living space may access the device, as well. When multiple individuals share a computing device, privacy related to the information on that device could be breached if safeguards are not in place. When individuals share devices, they should set up user accounts or provide certain privileges or permissions to ensure information is shared as intended.

Another consideration for navigating computing barriers during teleconsultation relates to consultees' comfort and familiarity with using computing technology as well as their ability to effectively problem solve computing barriers that go along with using various technology. We mentioned earlier in this text the benefits of consultees having repeated exposure to new technologies to increase acceptability, and you should also spend ample time patiently helping your consultees when computing barriers arise. When encountering barriers related to consultee comfort with technology, you can

(a) discuss with them why they may experience resistance and (b) propose alternative solutions that may better align with their comfort and values.

Last, as you interact with consultees, you might be prone to conduct much of their work through videoconference and be particularly susceptible to fatigue related to sitting in front of a screen interacting with individuals, while engaging in limited movement and contrasting environmental contexts. Consultees may also be susceptible to Zoom fatigue, especially if they provide educational supports to the student through remote access services (Bailenson, 2021). Regardless of the individual, all participants in the teleconsultation process have the potential to experience videoconference fatigue, and you should prioritize well-being activities to build resilient and sustainable habits in your practice. Some strategies to reduce videoconference fatigue and promote well-being include

- reducing blue light on screen displays
- taking short breaks to stretch or move your body
- scheduling 25- or 50-minute meetings in order to ensure break and transition time
- limiting synchronous videoconference meetings each day and trying not to overschedule

Technical Barriers

Some of the most common barriers that you and your consultees might experience during teleconsultation are those that are due to technical issues. Each teleconsultant and consultee will have varying competencies in navigating different technologies, and even the most proficient teleconsultant will experience technical issues during teleconsultation. We tend to experience a range of technical issues—everything from "You're on mute" and "Can you send me the videoconference link?" to dropped calls and lagged video/audio feeds. You should strive to be particularly familiar with how to troubleshoot technical barriers across videoconferencing platforms (e.g., Zoom, Google Meet, Microsoft Teams) and regularly check for software updates. Keeping the software current is a cumbersome effort—but necessary—and you should support your consultees with updating software, if needed. When new software becomes available, you should also take time to explore the updates and test out the functionality of the software, especially if a certain platform is new.

When working with technology and the inherent barriers that go along with using technology, be open to learning and problem solving. Most school districts have information technology departments with competent staff who can consult around technical issues. Throughout the teleconsultation

TABLE 8.1. Technical Considerations Impacting Rapport During Teleconsultation and Mitigation Strategies for Effective Rapport Building and Maintenance

Technical consideration	Mitigation strategy
Dropped videoconference	Have a phone number ready, and call the consultee on their preferred number
Low bandwidth (unstable audio/video)	Turn video off, stop screen sharing
Audio feedback/echo	Microphone and headphones
Videoconference software feature not available	Update software once per week
Recording	Inform consultee that video recording will occur, with permission

process, be patient with yourself and your students. Using technology can be an additional challenge, and ongoing learning to support and engage your consultees and students will prepare you to respond and sustain your teleconsultation practice. Any time you use or integrate a new technology, you should test the features before implementing it with consultees or students. You should plan for the worst but intend for the best—and have backup plans in place to maintain rapport and stay connected with the consultee(s) or student(s). Table 8.1 lists potential technical considerations that can impact rapport during the teleconsultation experience. Additionally, each consideration has an associated strategy to mitigate concern.

PLANNING AND ORGANIZATIONAL BARRIERS

As you practice within the respective organizations that you serve, barriers will arise that are related to the larger context of the teleconsultation services that are provided. These can relate to issues with the school/district administration or with the culture and community within the school. You should take the initiative to help support collaboration within the school community and between the school and community partners. Fostering a strong school–family–community partnership is beneficial for the student and the individuals who support the student. As a consultant, you are charged with supporting individuals or a team of people in a school system; you need to take the necessary steps to (a) understand the cultural context of where you are consulting and (b) seek out additional training to be culturally competent. Furthermore, by collaborating with the consultee and centering the voice of the student throughout, you help support a culturally relevant, effective, and acceptable support structure.

In Chapter 3, we discussed planning issues related to consultees missing meetings and contextualized those issues from an interpersonal perspective. In this section, we provide an alternative conceptualization for consultees missing meetings—this different perspective explains the missed meetings as due to the consultee having difficulty planning and managing competing demands. Many times, when consultees miss or no-show meetings, it is not necessarily related to poor rapport but is more about difficulty managing their busy schedules, dealing with competing demands, and responding to impromptu meetings. You should remember that consultees are trying their best with the skills and capacities that they currently have available. We can support these types of barriers by empathizing with these planning issues and reattempt to meet at a future date.

HIGH-INTENSITY BEHAVIOR AND CRISIS-RELATED BARRIERS

Teleconsultants who support schools will need to be prepared for instances of crisis, but at the student and school–community levels. These crises can include high-frequency or high-intensity behaviors of concern for specific students or impact multiple students, educators, and community members in crisis situations (e.g., gun violence, suicide, natural disaster). The challenges that you experience as a teleconsultant in all of these crisis situations are unique as compared with when you are supporting these same types of situations on-site. For example, as a teleconsultant, you are unable to physically support situations, as you are remotely joining the classroom or teleconsultation space. Because you are unable to physically support individuals due to those constraints, you need to plan procedures to ensure safety for the students, educators, and other partners who are participating in the teleconsultation experience. It is important to collaboratively plan for these potential circumstances, train with staff to build fluency on the planned procedures, and reassess and modify these plans as needed. Crisis responses should be planned and prescriptive in nature, so that people know how to respond, whom to get ahold of, and how to reach them (e.g., phone call, text message). If those plans are not in place, you may not be able to easily interface with the on-site school team and support crisis response efforts as necessary.

As part of the crisis support that teleconsultants provide to individual students, you may, at times, need to travel to be on-site. Some instances when you might need to attend in person are high-stakes meetings that require physical presence, or situations when remote methods of service delivery preclude you from effectively collaborating, coaching, or supporting the students and educators. When you support cases remotely, you should also be aware of the implications of including law enforcement during certain student-focused crisis responses. Not all first responders will have training in working with students with disabilities or in the teleconsultation process, and the mere presence of some responders (e.g., law enforcement) could trigger certain responses, based on previous negative experiences, from the students you are supporting. Increased school shootings in the past few decades have led to a higher presence of law enforcement in schools, which is contributing to the school-to-prison pipeline for marginalized students. Educational and community resources should be spent on school counselors, school psychologists, school social workers, and other support systems that provide prevention frameworks in these settings (R. King & Schindler, 2021).

TRAVEL BARRIERS

Another barrier that you could experience is the physical distance between the schools you serve, both within and across districts. Travel time is effectively eliminated with teleconsultation unless the situation calls for on-site support. A convenient aspect of teleconsultation is that because there is generally no travel, if someone forgets about a planned session or has a conflict that arises, you can quickly shift to a new task without being stuck en route to a new location. Although you benefit from reduced or eliminated travel, as it provides additional time for other tasks, caregivers also benefit from the reduced travel constraints. For example, there might be a caregiver who lives too far away from a school building or community center, which distance precludes them from meaningfully participating in a student services meeting such as an individualized education program meeting or a manifestation determination meeting. The teleconsultation process can disrupt the previously discussed barriers for those caregivers (and other community partners) to participate and collaborate in the process, despite geographical barriers.

CHILD CARE BARRIERS

Although the text talked mostly about educators as consultees, as the services expand to living spaces and caregiver consultees participate in the process, they will also be in the home, where other competing demands of child care may interfere with consultation meetings. Child care barriers are a reason why mental health professionals are unable to provide services, according to the American Academy of Child and Adolescent Psychiatry Committee on

Health Care Access and Economics Task Force on Mental Health (2009). Considering family and caregiver engagement, we can support families who have child care constraints by being able to meet them virtually in their living space. In certain scenarios, families are able to connect with school personnel only after school hours or when caregivers are responsible for child care for children in the living space. We can consider those barriers and provide support with more asynchronous content that is accessible on demand (as further discussed in Chapter 9), or we can find times within the day when child care constraints are less impactful.

Another contextual factor is that more students are staying online through their learning, as a result of exposure to online learning during the pandemic. In addition to the barriers of the consultee and the family that you are supporting, you may also have child care barriers from children studying from home and the competing demands in their living space. Traditionally, caregivers who have young children in their living space might have limited access to on-site meetings, but using teleconsultation could create accessible pathways to join meetings while fulfilling child care responsibilities (e.g., meeting during a nap).

HYBRID DELIVERY MODEL BARRIERS

We discussed presence earlier in the book (see Chapter 3), and when you consider the amount of presence you embody during the teleconsultation process, you must attempt to benefit all online participants. With some consultees joining remotely and others on-site in the educational space, you will need to ensure equitable opportunities for engagement, depending on who is joining remotely. This is especially important when high-stakes meetings occur. The individuals who are online might feel isolated or disconnected from those attending in person, and individuals who are in person should make active attempts to include participants joining remotely.

At times, you may need to practice in person and at other times online; however, we need to understand the extent to which a hybrid format of teleconsultation is feasible and sustainable. Teleconsultation can be an augmentative tool to traditional consultation and has benefits. For example, you might be attending a meeting that goes past the ending time and are therefore unable to make it to another meeting on time, at a school 20 minutes away. In a scenario such as this, consultants can become teleconsultants and use their technology tools in a hybrid fashion. This model is more reactive teleconsultation than practice, but if you have strong rapport with your consultee, it may be easier to use a hybrid teleconsultation model. Also, the hybrid model could be more supportive to consultees, as teleconsultants can provide blended supports, especially when in-person services are necessary to advance rapport or to effectively model a skill or assess a behavior of concern. You might consider a hybrid mode (i.e., more on-site supports) if your consultee has never engaged in teleconsultation and seems apprehensive with interfacing through that modality.

The consultee may also experience barriers to hybrid delivery models in their own profession if they are teaching online or using a combination of in-person and remote methods. Although synchronous hybrid learning is not necessarily considered the most effective method, due to several pedagogical and technological issues, many educators may find themselves in this situation due to extraneous variables. The National Education Association (2021) provides considerations such as balancing synchronous/ asynchronous learning, being transparent with expectations, communicating deadlines and accommodations, and using a flipped classroom model. As a teleconsultant, you can provide support for teachers by helping train consultees in their communicative, didactic, and digital competencies and by collaborating on the creation of engaging and autonomous learning content (Lorenzo-Lledó et al., 2021). Collaboration with the consultee to pursue the best practices and considerations will determine successful implementation of the hybrid model. Raes and colleagues' (2019) systematic review of synchronous hybrid learning echoed similar considerations regarding training and support, clear communication, and curriculum alignment. Some of their suggestions for successful implementation of the hybrid model include the following:

- assign students roles such as "chat tracker" or "technology troubleshooter"
- train students and teachers to handle technology
- explicitly state expectations for students and what teachers can expect
- use polls, quizzes, breakout rooms, and open-ended questions to engage students
- use a flipped classroom approach to blend synchronous and asynchronous material

PRIVACY AND SECURITY BARRIERS

During the teleconsultation process, privacy and security barriers pose significant challenges; however, you should feel confident that you can address those barriers through thoughtful and cautious considerations for your teleconsultation practice, as discussed in Chapter 2. One issue related to privacy and security relates to school district or caregiver apprehension around recording content. The option to record content is not necessary for teleconsultation, and you can choose to have synchronous videoconference sessions without recording. You can work with school partners and caregivers to notify them of the teleconsultation process and explain (a) how no data are stored when video content is not recorded and (b) that the synchronous observations are practically similar to in-person observation of students. Using legally compliant software also adds a crucial layer of security to ensure consultee and student data are protected. Obtaining partner buy-in through transparency and assurances of security and privacy will be important as you build trust and collaboration.

Another privacy barrier relates to the availability of a physical space where the consultee can engage in secure teleconsultation. For instance, there could be multiple students and other educators present when sessions take place in a school. The presence of such other individuals could lead to breaches of privacy and confidentiality, an event that the consultee may perceive as aversive. In this situation, consultants can offer specific guidance to consultees on ways to modify their environment to preserve the confidential nature of information discussed during meetings (Peterson et al., 2019).

SOCIAL VALIDITY

When you consider the context of the barriers that you might experience during the teleconsultation process, you should look at those issues systemically rather than attempting to assign blame to an individual or perceiving the consultee as having bad intentions in their interactions. If teleconsultants bring bias into their process of dealing with barriers and are not looking systemically at the barriers, they run the risk of oppressing their students (or consultees), either explicitly or implicitly.

As consultants, we aim to produce socially valid outcomes with our consultees in order to support students, but we must be cautious not to be myopic in this process. Of course, improving outcomes is central to the teleconsultation work; however, despite the established link between treatment integrity and treatment outcomes (DiGennaro et al., 2005; Sanetti & Collier-Meek, 2017), consultees may find it challenging to sufficiently adhere to treatment procedures in school and home settings. Remember that this is commonplace, as you will have limited ability, as a teleconsultant, to influence circumstances outside of the school building. Further, all students', consultees', and teleconsultants' experiences outside of the school building—in the living space or community—influence what happens inside of the building. As the teleconsultant working in the larger support system, you should always approach the work from a place of support and strive to shape skills and enhance motivation, so that all individuals can experience a fulfilling life.

9 FUTURE DIRECTIONS IN SCHOOL TELECONSULTATION

Using teleconsultation services to support educators, students, and their families has foundational support through research, and, as evidenced through the rapid service delivery changes that took place during the global COVID-19 pandemic, this service provision modality has solid and sustainable applications beyond the pandemic and as another tool that school consultants can use. Considering that teleconsultation is still a relatively new practice area, there are many viable opportunities for researchers and practitioners alike to use these technologies to test the limits of what is possible, as well as areas that we need to explore and understand as we expand which types of services are delivered.

There are many different directions to go from here; the future research and practice of teleconsultation must highlight the diverse work that is in the field. As a teleconsultant, you are making decisions regarding the hardware and software to incorporate into your practice as well as the existing evidence for various populations and referral concerns. When contending with future directions, there are still gaps in evaluating not only teleconsultation processes and outcomes but also social validity. Much of the extant

https://doi.org/10.1037/0000366-009
Teleconsultation in Schools: A Guide to Collaborative Practice, by A. J. Fischer and B. S. Bloomfield
Copyright © 2024 by the American Psychological Association. All rights reserved.

literature does not explore maintenance and generalization effects of teleconsultation. Although this chapter highlights some of the innovative future directions for teleconsultation, the field is constantly evolving to align with best practices, the most recent technological developments, and current barriers to effective service delivery. Thus, we cannot discuss all innovations, but the process to evaluate and incorporate novel applications is the same: Use sound methodologies to test out whether it works for you and your students.

There are some important distinctions between applied practice and research in teleconsultation. For researchers in the field, it is imperative to clearly document details of the hardware, software, populations, and teleconsultation processes. This will help with replication of published studies as well as expand our understanding of the evidence base for teleconsultation—for whom does teleconsultation best offer support, and under what circumstances is it effective? When is it not effective? When should you defer to in-person models of service delivery? For the teleconsultants, data-based decision making is still core to the problem-solving process; we use a decision-making matrix (see Chapter 7) to assess whether we have met the stated goals, and we gather information from various partners to determine whether the process and targeted outcomes are acceptable and effective. These same considerations should be used for new technological features: Use relevant data to test out whether the feature is effective, efficient, and acceptable to the consultees and students with whom you work.

The field of psychology is said to have a *replication crisis*, or a crisis of low rates of replicability of studies in the field. Many of the key works in the field have not been independently demonstrated to have the same or similar effects. In psychological research, there are rates as high as 36%, like many other areas of social sciences (Open Science Collaboration, 2015). In a review of publication trends in the top education journals, less than 1% of studies were classified as replications across 5 years (Makel & Plucker, 2014). Within the body of school teleconsultation literature, there are still a lot of unanswered questions and emerging research. For example, H. C. King and colleagues (2021) identified, through their systematic review, what has currently been studied in this area. As all of those articles were single-case research demonstrating different interventions and outcomes, there are still areas in which we need to expand our work yet not forget to verify the findings of some of what has already been demonstrated.

This chapter outlines considerations for future research and practice in teleconsultation. We hope that readers will be inspired by the potential for this service modality and integrate teleconsultation into their practice in order to continue to support service delivery efforts. It is important to note that teleconsultation is an emerging area of practice; many of the future directions described later in this chapter are not well established in the research but have much potential to impact research, teaching, and practice. Despite the potential benefits of much of this technology, teleconsultation researchers, practitioners, and trainers should be extremely cautious about using those strategies.

In machine learning and automation of tasks, for example, there is bias related to using algorithms, and algorithms reflect the learning context of the individuals who programmed the code. Any bias within the programming and subsequent classifications or coding could be disproportionately applied, referred to as *digital redlining*, which creates inequities for students (Gilliard & Culik, 2019). This extends to other new technologies that may not be equally effective or relevant across groups of students. Prior to implementing any new technology, researchers and practitioners need to carefully consider any limitations, biases, and restrictions of that technology when applying it in their work with vulnerable people. There is a need to integrate the next generation of technology, some examples of which we discuss in this chapter, into the school teleconsultation research sector. The following sections highlight applications of current technology for trainers, practitioners, and researchers—we delineate the content by synchronous and asynchronous applications. As new technologies are developed, further applications may emerge.

APPLICATIONS IN SYNCHRONOUS TELECONSULTATION

The commercially available hardware and software to collect audio and video information have been progressing rapidly. As the technology continues to improve and users access these technologies, teleconsultants will be able to enjoy the benefits of robust and readily available tools to enhance the synchronous teleconsultation process. In the following subsections, we discuss some of the potential applications for synchronous and face-to-face consultation, including video capturing devices, telepresence robots, aerial drones, wearable devices, and access to interpreter services.

Video Capturing Devices

Camera type and quality is one area of technology that has seen significant improvement. Several recent developments with 360° cameras and video recording now allow everyday consumers to record a 360° video; this better captures all motion within sight of the camera than has been possible with traditional ones. A smartphone camera angle is approximately 120°. By capturing a full circle, the observer can track a student as they move about an environment.

Alternative developments include ease of use for multiple camera angles. Multiple camera angles have been commonplace on the small and big screens for decades; this is how the camera can jump from one person to another when different people are talking or continue to follow an action scene in motion. This also could be of great use in behavior observations, where one camera can be positioned to capture the students and a second can be targeted on the teacher. When the camera recordings are aligned, a teleconsultant can then simultaneously code student and teacher behavior and ensure that all actions are captured. With multiple cameras, you can also capture multiple audio channels. Again, this has been a feature of the film industry but has not had much exposure in the school setting. A teleconsultant can capture a student's and teacher's audio feeds, which can better capture information.

Multiple camera angles can also be applied to the teleconsultant; using synchronous technologies, the teleconsultant is often modeling intervention procedures, collecting data, or sharing information while also talking with the consultee. Similar to how the screen share function can be applied to talk with a consultee and share information on a screen, more than one camera can be used to provide alternative viewpoints (e.g., front and side angle, front and above angle) when modeling intervention procedures. While a forward-facing angle gives the consultee a mirrorlike model, a side profile or above angle may help the observer get a better understanding of body positioning or specific procedures to engage in the specified task. The camera setup can include several cameras connected to one device or can use multiple devices; a smartphone or tablet can often sign in to the same meeting and act as a second camera for purposes of modeling. When signing in the second device, ensure that the microphone is disabled, as two separate devices in close physical proximity may result in echo or audio feedback.

Telepresence Robots

The aforementioned technologies increase the teleconsultant's view when conducting teleconsultation; 360° cameras increase the field of view from one stationary location, whereas using multiple cameras provides separate viewing angles from which to observe behavior within a space. As an alternative to these viewing modifications described, teleconsultants can use other hardware, such as telepresence robots, to dynamically observe behavior within an environment (Bloomfield et al., 2020; Zoder-Martell et al., 2020). A telepresence robot is a type of hardware that incorporates device movement into the teleconsultation experience (Fischer et al., 2018). In many cases, you can remotely control the camera and screen. Some telepresence robots are on a stationary base, and you can adjust the angle of observation (e.g., Kubi), whereas others you can drive or move around spaces in schools, including classrooms, hallways, and so on (e.g., Double).

Using telepresence robots allows you to increase your level of presence, and as technology improves, we will be able to engage with the consultee with greater presence (Fischer, Collins, et al., 2019). With current commercially available technology, you should consider using telepresence robots to navigate physical spaces and engage with consultees and students, especially when working with multiple consultees within a school building. These presence-enhancing technologies can also be useful in nonschool spaces, such as the community or living spaces, and with permission from families or caregivers, you could use telepresence robots to support students—and the generalization and maintenance of skills—in various environments.

Aerial Drones

The classroom environment is not the only setting in which teleconsultants would practice in schools: The playground, gymnasium, and hallways can also be settings in which to provide support and consultation. While telepresence robots may nicely support some of these environments, many of the commercially available telepresence robots are designed to be indoors on flat surfaces and within proximity to Wi-Fi. Some of these alternative settings might not be as accessible due to uneven terrain, steps, or distance from stable Wi-Fi. An alternative technology that may best address this need, particularly in outdoor recreational environments, is the camera-enabled aerial drone. This device is a remote-controlled, flying camera that can operate across greater distances; however, the drone does need to remain within line of sight to the controller. Drones are a feasible alternative to conducting behavior observations in larger outdoor environments such as playgrounds (H. C. King et al., 2020). H. C. King and colleagues (2020) conducted a preliminary proof of concept that drones can be used to capture video of children playing on a playground in a comparable manner to on-the-ground video recordings. An added benefit of the aerial drone is that it can move to follow a specific child and remain at a greater distance from the child than other methods allow. However, the propeller noise of the drone may be noticeable to some students, and observations are limited in duration by the battery capacity (not exceeding 25 minutes in most consumer drones).

With those limitations in mind, you want to remember that a drone can get an aerial viewpoint that is not inhibited by playground equipment or other surface-level obstacles.

Wearable Devices

Wearable technologies are devices that the user has on a part of their body, and those technologies provide information or services to the user. For example, many smartwatches provide information about messages, play music, answer calls, and control other devices. Similarly, these smartwatches can collect biometric and environmental data, such as heart rate, decibel level, audio recordings, steps taken, and distance traveled. Smartglasses are another example of wearable technology; these also have a variety of features, such as the ability to project a small display onto the lens, record audio and video, capture some biometric data, and project audio notifications.

These and other wearable technologies can be used in the teleconsultation sector. Smartwatches (e.g., Apple Watch) have been used for providing in-the-moment coaching and performance feedback for educators (e.g., Markelz et al., 2019; White et al., 2022). On these devices, the teleconsultant can deliver a tactile prompt (i.e., vibration), with or without textual feedback (e.g., a text message on screen), during coaching sessions. The discreet feedback can inform the teacher or staff member what they should do next or what they are doing well and would not be noticed or seen by the student with whom they are working.

Beyond feedback, these devices can be used for data collection. As previously mentioned, many smartwatches have built-in sensors that can automatically collect a variety of data. One key feature is the built-in accelerometer, or a sensor that measures changes in velocity over time. This sensor can measure changes in movement, such as the movement associated with aggression or disruptive behavior. These wearable devices have been demonstrated to automate this data collection of behaviors of concern using the built-in accelerometers (e.g., Plötz et al., 2012).

Access to Interpretation Services

One of the earlier applications of telehealth to medical practice was using interpreters to enable services for students who speak a different language than their provider (Masland et al., 2010). While much of this support continues to be used with the provider and the student in the same physical space, teleconsultation can be used to provide interpretation services for others who also are communicating across telehealth. These technologies are especially useful for less frequently spoken languages or for smaller communities, where finding an appropriate and qualified interpreter is difficult. As other technological advancements continue, there may be novel applications for interpretation services to change and improve with other aspects of teleconsultation. For example, Siri, the voice assistant on Apple products, released a real-time translation platform where she can translate audio into 11 languages. This technology can be further expanded and improved to offer simultaneous interpretation of multiple languages for participating parties in the conversation.

APPLICATIONS IN ASYNCHRONOUS TELECONSULTATION

Some of the current applications of asynchronous teleconsultation are only as limited as the hardware and software capabilities—as processors get faster and more efficient, and internet connectivity gets faster and more reliable, many of the subsequent applications will be easier to use and more frequently accessed in practice. As internet security improves with more advanced and more efficient encryption standards, the ongoing practices will become faster, safer, and more secure. Today, compression standards impose limits on the size of files that can be shared and the quality of those files; these compression standards are constantly evolving to allow everyday users to share higher quality video in smaller and smaller files.

The added benefit of this expansion of computing capabilities is improved functionality. Artificial intelligence will continue expanding into this space, with more chatbots that are humanistic and virtual interactions with a computer. For some questions, and guidance, these platforms can function as virtual consultants to provide ongoing support in a virtual environment. Virtual assistants (e.g., Siri, Alexa, Google Assistant) have proliferated the smart home environment, providing information, notifications, and vocal assistance to control lights, music, TV, and other hardware around the home. When connected with other sensors, these systems can act as a hub to provide information and control devices based on the weather (e.g., rain sensors), your location (e.g., GPS), movement (e.g., motion sensors), or the position of windows and doors (e.g., contact sensors). These chatbots have already been used in the health care and education industries, with providing patient follow-up care, mental health support, and education information (Bhirud et al., 2019; Pérez et al., 2020). As these technologies are further developed for the education sector, these virtual teleconsultants can provide educators tips on implementation fidelity, answer frequently asked questions, offer guidance on next steps, and inform educators when they should seek out further support from the teleconsultant.

Machine Learning

Machine learning is a type of artificial intelligence that refers to a computing system's ability to learn information from data, recognize patterns, and make decisions or conclusions about novel data. The process of machine learning functions with minimal human interaction; however, individuals who use machine learning apply those decisions to relevant outcomes related to their day-to-day responsibilities.

There is currently limited research in implementing machine learning into the teleconsultant's daily practice. As we begin to integrate machine learning into our services, we can relieve ourselves of responsibilities that would otherwise take considerable time, which allows us more time to spend with consultees or on developing or evaluating the intervention. Automating specific tasks is an application of machine learning, and you could use automation with time-intensive tasks, such as data collection and observation coding, to increase your (or the consultee's) efficiency. For example, teleconsultants who use automation applied to direct observations of students can use software to complete those tasks, rather than spending significant time conducting behavior observations, coding the observation data, and graphing the data. The automation process can be used to quickly complete many of those tasks, and the teleconsultant could focus their consultative effort on analyzing and interpreting the data, coaching and providing performance feedback to the consultee, or collaborating with community partners and caregivers.

Further developments in automation can facilitate data collection and analysis procedures as well. In general, increased capacity for automation can be adapted to many of the coding and analysis procedures that teleconsultants may seek to use. For example, increased accuracy in automatic transcription and translation software will make it easier for teleconsultants to review information discussed during a meeting and communicate with others who speak a different language than the teleconsultant. This information is often needed for researchers who may want to analyze what was said during these meetings—in other words, assess the teleconsultation process. Fischer and colleagues (2017) utilized the consultation analysis record for analyzing verbalizations during videoconferencing interviews, which is a tool that is used to assess for key content and process variables during consultation interviews. They adapted the traditional paper-and-pencil format of the evaluation tool to a spreadsheet-based procedure that helps automate some of the process, which was helpful in saving time and providing quicker analyses of the effectiveness of the interview. Future developments in this computerized tool can have many applications to training and practice as well (e.g., Erchul et al., 2018).

Video Recording for Supervision and Feedback

Telesupervision refers to the use of technology in place of in-person supervision. According to Sellers and Walker (2019), the use of telesupervision, as opposed to typical supervision, may be due to challenges in scheduling, geographical distance, and the complexity of overseeing trainees. Technology has become so efficient that it may be beneficial to use telesupervision even when typical supervision is available. Videoconferencing is one of many means of telesupervision—but it is, arguably, one of the most prominent in recent years. It allows the supervisor and supervisee to see and interact with each other in real time. Consider adhering to the following three pillars when using telesupervision: best interest, transparency, and collaboration (Rousmaniere, 2014). This is to ensure that telesupervision is not used simply for convenience but is administered in an ethical and intentional manner.

Teleconsultation trainers should consider using video-recorded self-evaluation and feedback software, such as Lyssn or GoReact. Trainers can use these tools to provide time-stamped feedback to supervisees and use embedded technologies to build competencies in therapeutic skills, such as motivational interviewing skills, active listening, and affirmations (in the case of Lyssn; Imel et al., 2017; Tanana et al., 2019).

Teleconsultants should also consider using web- and app-based recording tools such as Flip, which allows users to engage with easily accessible video recordings. Teleconsultants can record messages to consultees or caregivers, and vice versa, allowing opportunities for asynchronous communication while maintaining a face-to-face element to the interaction.

Written Communication to Stay Connected

Although there are some studies showing the benefit of using written communication to provide consultees feedback and support implementation efforts (Fallon et al., 2015), future research needs to help teleconsultants understand the consultees' written communication modality preferences and help inform which communication platforms allow for the best collaboration between team members. Options include email, text message, and messaging apps. However, whichever options teleconsultants select, they need to ensure that they have a business associate agreement with the developers. These steps will help to safeguard protected information.

APPLICATIONS IN TRAINING TELECONSULTANTS

Many of the applications discussed thus far can be adapted to multiple contexts. For example, increased automation will support better synchronous and asynchronous teleconsultation practices. Across research and practice, many of these applications have been focused on teleconsultation outcomes or processes; however, we must not forget how we use these technologies to better train the next generation of teleconsultants. The following information describes applications for training teleconsultants and highlights contemporary technologies that include machine learning and virtual/augmented reality learning environments.

The use of machine learning in automated data collection and analysis is one of the easiest applications that can be used to better train practitioners; when practitioners can access immediate feedback on their process and outcomes, they can make in-the-moment changes to how they communicate with others. Erchul et al. (2018) discussed the ways in which the consultation analysis record has been, and will continue to be, a useful tool for trainers to assess the effectiveness of problem-solving consultation meetings. By increasing the efficiency of the data coding and analysis process, trainers can provide better feedback to trainees.

Beyond the advances in computing, other technologies such as virtual reality (VR) and augmented reality (AR) can offer training scenarios not otherwise available to trainees. VR can be used with scenarios that are not feasible or frequent enough to offer training opportunities. In scenarios of high-intensity or higher risk behaviors, a trainee might have fewer opportunities to rehearse in these contexts. Thus, a virtual environment where a simulated scenario can be projected in a realistic manner can allow for rehearsal and performance feedback before entering those scenarios in practice. Additionally, through live rehearsals or video recordings, the trainer can provide high-quality feedback to the trainee. Although VR and AR technologies for training and professional learning are in the early stages, teleconsultants will be able to use these technologies in their practice in the near future. Mursion's TeachLivE is a simulated learning environment designed for teachers to develop essential skills for the classroom (Ledger et al., 2019). As mentioned earlier, the benefits of mixed-reality classroom simulations are that educators can rehearse high-intensity and high-risk scenarios in a controlled environment, free of consequences.

As with VR and AR, advances in programmable robotics will have more applications in the simulated training space and are showing promise as a tool for training and professional learning. Programmable humanoid robots provide an approximative rehearsal environment for trainees, where the trainee can see and interact with the robot in humanlike manners in real time. Some examples of this work exist in applied behavior analysis, where researchers use socially assistive robots (SARs) to deliver robot-mediated interventions to improve social skills for individuals with autism spectrum disorder. The SARs were able to emulate the behaviors of human therapists during a listening comprehension intervention, which improved the participants' ability to answer wh-questions (Louie et al., 2020).

RESEARCH APPLICATIONS

Future applications for school teleconsultation include different presenting concerns, with broader and more diverse participants within the consultative continuum of services. If the premise of school teleconsultation is to increase access and accessibility to support and services in underserved schools, then continued research efforts should intentionally address this through their recruitment of participants and presentation of results. Through increased presentation of ongoing work in this space, we can demonstrate how many people are impacted through applied research and practice.

Report the Participants in the Sample

One of the limitations discussed in H. C. King et al.'s (2021) systematic review of school teleconsultation was that there were gaps in reporting participant demographics—most of the included participants were reported to be white males. While many studies included students with disabilities, many of those studies did not report any description of student diagnosis or classification. Of the studies that reported these characteristics, many reported providing teleconsultation services to support students with a developmental delay or who were on the autism spectrum. While the H. C. King et al. (2021) review is only one example, there is more that needs to be done. First, by clearly reporting consultant, consultee, and student demographics, researchers can help show what works and for whom. Problem-solving teleconsultation is an effective framework, but without future research to understand the nuances of this model, teleconsultants will not be able to adapt their services to be culturally responsive and sustaining with various communities. Future researchers and practitioners of school teleconsultation should include broader samples of diverse participants within the consultative continuum of services.

Test the Limits of Teleconsultation

Much of the extant literature on school teleconsultation focuses on the immediate impact of teleconsultation practices on behavior change for an individual student. A school teleconsultant may engage in many other types of work, and by testing the limits of school teleconsultation, we can better understand the depth and breadth of this field of work. Some aspects that teleconsultant researchers could consider while testing the limits of teleconsultation include (a) evaluating the effectiveness and acceptability of teleconsultation to address various presenting problems, (b) assessing the adequacy of teleconsultation to meet the needs of differing consultees (e.g., general education teachers, parents) supporting the student in different settings (e.g., home, community, area of school), and (c) adjusting the levels of presence and amount of synchronous support available in order to enhance the face-to-face synchronous meetings.

Other gaps in the literature include the ongoing maintenance of behavior change and the generalizability of the skills taught to the consultee. To address both questions, researchers need to extend the time in which they are assessing behavior change. For generalization, it is still unknown whether a teacher can apply the skills taught from teleconsultation to a different group of students or in a different context. Similarly, is the behavior change sustained over time? Without explicit measurement of generalization and maintenance, we are unable to understand the implementation factors that will sustain the practices.

The last gap that we identified in the literature pertains to the need for teleconsultation research to include consultation collaboration through family, school, and community partnerships. Currently, the teleconsultation literature only shows effectiveness and acceptability with teacher consultees, and caregivers have not been included in the teleconsultation process as explicitly. Teleconsultants should prioritize high-quality family–school partnerships, and researchers need to explore the benefits of family–school partnerships in teleconsultation. Future work on these partnerships should build off of the strong foundational work within conjoint behavioral consultation (Garbacz, 2020; Sheridan, Welch, & Orme, 1996) and leverage strong family–school partnerships through contemporary technology (Fischer & Bloomfield, 2020).

Supporting Online Learning

Although not a new modality for education, online learning has become increasingly popular and practical due to the COVID-19 pandemic. Many school districts have developed their own online K–12 schools to meet local needs. As such, there will be an ongoing demand to support students who engage in online learning, and being able to support students who learn in this format must be intentionally targeted through training, research, and practice. Because teleconsultation to support online learners will need to focus on engagement, teleconsultants who support these learners will need to engage not only the students but also their caregivers because the education will be received in the student's living space rather than a classroom. What follows are two examples of ways that teleconsultants can consider increasing student engagement for online learning, which we contextualize through the multitiered system of support.

When teleconsultants support educators with their online classrooms (i.e., universal support for all students), they will need to incorporate data collection methods that use relevant constructs to verify student engagement. Videoconferencing applications are positioned well to link with software that can record when students enter keystrokes, turn cameras on/off, write text in the chat, or respond with emoji reactions. Educators and teleconsultants alike can use the engagement data to understand which students are more engaged and which are less—or not at all—engaged. Subsequently, teleconsultants and educators can use those data to differentiate their instruction, particularly engagement strategies, to meet the needs of all students. At the end of each teaching session, daily, or weekly, the educator can interact with a web-based learning dashboard that provides summative data on student engagement. Educators can provide more engagement opportunities for students who are less engaged and consider Tier 2 strategies for increasing academic engagement, such as virtual adaptation of the check-in, check-out intervention (Hawken, 2020).

In an online learning setting, Tier 2 interventions might include a caregiver component, if they are available, to support the intervention implementation. Including caregivers in the intervention process underscores the need for teleconsultants to engage in conjoint behavioral teleconsultation to support online educators, students, and their caregivers. In this online education format, when the teleconsultant is involved, they should continue to bridge the relationship between the caregiver and the educator. If family members are working from home, teleconsultants could connect with them to see whether they are able to provide feedback to the child at a scheduled interval. If the student does not have a caregiver who can support, the teleconsultant could work with the consultee to schedule digital reminders or emails for the student so that the consultee can check in on engagement, ask questions, or request support.

CONCLUSION

With technology advancing at exponential rates, the applications of teleconsultation are practically endless, if there are interested practitioners, researchers, and trainers who are willing to use these tools in their respective domains. With the foundational content described in the text, teleconsultants can begin to feel comfortable embarking on their teleconsultation practice, while being intentional about how they engage in the practice. At its core, school teleconsultation is a framework for problem solving in a culturally responsive and collaborative manner using technology, while using a clear decision-making process with a constant consideration of the ethical, legal, and professional implications of the work. Through teleconsultation, school consultants can provide, to a wider population, increased access to their services. When incorporating novel teleconsultation applications into practice, teleconsultants should stay abreast of emerging innovations and research in that area in order to support the next generation of school teleconsultants.

References

Abidin, R. R. (1997). Parenting Stress Index: A measure of the parent–child system. In C. P. Zalaquett & R. J. Wood (Eds.), *Evaluating stress: A book of resources* (pp. 277–291). Scarecrow Education.

Alpert, J. L. (1976). Conceptual bases of mental health consultation in the schools. *Professional Psychology, 7*(4), 619–626. https://doi.org/10.1037/h0078612

American Academy of Child and Adolescent Psychiatry Committee on Health Care Access and Economics Task Force on Mental Health. (2009). Improving mental health services in primary care: Reducing administrative and financial barriers to access and collaboration. *Pediatrics, 123*(4), 1248–1251. https://doi.org/10.1542/peds.2009-0048

American Psychological Association. (2017). *Ethical principles of psychologists and code of conduct* (2002, amended effective June 1, 2010, and January 1, 2017). https://www.apa.org/ethics/code/index.aspx

Bailenson, J. N. (2021). Nonverbal overload: A theoretical argument for the causes of Zoom fatigue. *Technology, Mind, and Behavior, 2*(1). Advance online publication. https://doi.org/10.1037/tmb0000030

Barretto, A., Wacker, D. P., Harding, J., Lee, J., & Berg, W. K. (2006). Using telemedicine to conduct behavioral assessments. *Journal of Applied Behavior Analysis, 39*(3), 333–340. https://doi.org/10.1901/jaba.2006.173-04

Baum, D. D., & Lane, J. R. (1976). An application of the "bug-in-the-ear" communication system for training psychometrists. *Counselor Education and Supervision, 15*(4), 309–310. https://doi.org/10.1002/j.1556-6978.1976.tb02010.x

Behavior Analyst Certification Board. (2020). *Ethics code for behavior analysts*. https://www.bacb.com/wp-content/bacb-compliance-code-future

Belar, C. D. (1998). Graduate education in clinical psychology: "We're not in Kansas anymore." *American Psychologist, 53*(4), 456–464. https://doi.org/10.1037/0003-066X.53.4.456

Belser, C. T., Shillingford, M. A., & Joe, J. R. (2016). The ASCA model and a multi-tiered system of supports: A framework to support students of color with problem behavior. *The Professional Counselor, 6*(3), 251–262. https://doi.org/10.15241/cb.6.3.251

Bergan, J., & Caldwell, T. (1967). Operant techniques in school psychology. *Psychology in the Schools, 4*(2), 136–141. https://doi.org/10.1002/1520-6807(196704)4:2<136::AID-PITS2310040208>3.0.CO;2-O

Bhirud, N., Tataale, S., Randive, S., & Nahar, S. (2019). A literature review on chatbots in healthcare domain. *International Journal of Scientific & Technology Research, 8*(7), 225–231.

Blom-Hoffman, J., & Rose, G. S. (2007). Applying motivational interviewing to school-based consultation: A commentary on "Has Consultation Achieved Its Primary Prevention Potential?," an article by Joseph E. Zins. *Journal of Educational and Psychological Consultation, 17*(2–3), 151–156. https://doi.org/10.1080/10474410701346451

Bloomfield, B. S., Fischer, A. J., King, H. C., Lehman, E. L., & Clark, R. R. (2020). Exploring implementor error during remotely conducted school-based functional analysis telehealth training package. *Journal of Applied School Psychology, 36*(4), 347–375. https://doi.org/10.1080/15377903.2020.1749204

Bowles, P. E., & Nelson, R. O. (1976). Training teachers as mediators: Efficacy of a workshop versus the bug-in-the-ear technique. *Journal of School Psychology, 14*(1), 15–26. https://doi.org/10.1016/0022-4405(76)90058-3

Brown, J. M., Naser, S. C., Brown Griffin, C., Grapin, S. L., & Proctor, S. L. (2022). A multicultural, gender, and sexually diverse affirming school-based consultation framework. *Psychology in the Schools, 59*, 14–33. https://doi.org/10.1002/pits.22593

Caplan, G., & Caplan, R. B. (1999). *Mental health consultation and collaboration*. Waveland Press.

Chafouleas, S. M., Briesch, A. M., Riley-Tillman, T. C., Christ, T. J., Black, A. C., & Kilgus, S. P. (2010). An investigation of the generalizability and dependability of Direct Behavior Rating Single Item Scales (DBR-SIS) to measure academic engagement and disruptive behavior of middle school students. *Journal of School Psychology, 48*(3), 219–246. https://doi.org/10.1016/j.jsp.2010.02.001

Chin, W. W., Johnson, N. A., & Schwarz, A. (2008). A fast form approach to measuring technology acceptance and other constructs. *Management Information Systems Quarterly, 32*(4), 687–703. https://doi.org/10.2307/25148867

Clopton, K. L., & Knesting, K. (2006). Rural school psychology: Re-opening the discussion. *Journal of Research in Rural Education, 21*(5), 1–11. https://jrre.psu.edu/sites/default/files/2019-08/21-5.pdf

Coffey, A. L., Shawler, L. A., Jessel, J., Nye, M. L., Bain, T. A., & Dorsey, M. F. (2020). Interview-informed synthesized contingency analysis (IISCA): Novel interpretations and future directions. *Behavior Analysis in Practice, 13*(1), 217–225. https://doi.org/10.1007/s40617-019-00348-3

Collins, T. A., & Hawkins, R. O. (Eds.). (2021). *Peers as change agents: A guide to implementing peer-mediated interventions in schools*. Oxford University Press.

Coutinho, J., Ribeiro, E., Hill, C., & Safran, J. (2011). Therapists' and clients' experiences of alliance ruptures: A qualitative study. *Psychotherapy Research, 21*(5), 525–540. https://doi.org/10.1080/10503307.2011.587469

Cox, D. J., Plavnick, J. B., & Brodhead, M. T. (2020). A proposed process for risk mitigation during the COVID-19 pandemic. *Behavior Analysis in Practice, 13*(2), 299–305. https://doi.org/10.1007/s40617-020-00430-1

Cuticelli, M., Collier-Meek, M., & Coyne, M. (2016). Increasing the quality of Tier 1 reading instruction: Using performance feedback to increase opportunities to respond during implementation of a core reading program. *Psychology in the Schools, 53*(1), 89–105. https://doi.org/10.1002/pits.21884

Dart, E. H., Cook, C. R., Collins, T. A., Gresham, F. M., & Chenier, J. S. (2012). Test driving interventions to increase treatment integrity and student outcomes. *School Psychology Review, 41*(4), 467–481. https://doi.org/10.1080/02796015.2012.12087500

Dawson, M., Cummings, J. A., Harrison, P. L., Short, R. J., Gorin, S., & Palomares, R. (2004). The 2002 multisite Conference on the Future of School Psychology: Next steps. *School Psychology Review, 33*(1), 115–125. https://doi.org/10.1080/02796015.2004.12086235

Delgado, C., Gonzalez-Gordon, R. G., Aragón, E., & Navarro, J. I. (2017). Different methods for long-term systematic assessment of challenging behaviors in people with severe intellectual disability. *Frontiers in Psychology, 8*, 17. https://doi.org/10.3389/fpsyg.2017.00017

Demers, J. A., & Sullivan, A. L. (2016). Confronting the ubiquity of electronic communication and social media: Ethical and legal considerations for psychoeducational practice. *Psychology in the Schools, 53*(5), 517–532. https://doi.org/10.1002/pits.21920

DiGennaro, F. D., Martens, B. K., & Kleinmann, A. E. (2007). A comparison of performance feedback procedures on teachers' treatment implementation integrity and students' inappropriate behavior in special education classrooms. *Journal of Applied Behavior Analysis, 40*(3), 447–461. https://doi.org/10.1901/jaba.2007.40-447

DiGennaro, F. D., Martens, B. K., & McIntyre, L. L. (2005). Increasing treatment integrity through negative reinforcement: Effects on teacher and student behavior. *School Psychology Review, 34*(2), 220–231. https://doi.org/10.1080/02796015.2005.12086284

Dunbar, R. I. M. (2017). Breaking bread: The functions of social eating. *Adaptive Human Behavior and Physiology, 3*(3), 198–211. https://doi.org/10.1007/s40750-017-0061-4

Elliott, S. N., & Treuting, M. V. (1991). The Behavior Intervention Rating Scale: Development and validation of a pretreatment acceptability and effectiveness measure. *Journal of School Psychology, 29*(1), 43–51. https://doi.org/10.1016/0022-4405(91)90014-I

Ennis, R. P., Royer, D. J., Lane, K. L., & Dunlap, K. D. (2020). Behavior-specific praise in pre-K–12 settings: Mapping the 50-year knowledge base. *Behavioral Disorders, 45*(3), 131–147. https://doi.org/10.1177/0198742919843075

Erchul, W. P. (1987). *Consultant Evaluation Form (CEF)* [Database record]. APA PsycTests. https://doi.org/10.1037/t00871-000

Erchul, W. P., Fischer, A. J., Collier-Meek, M. A., & Bloomfield, B. S. (2018). Highlighting the utility of the Consultation Analysis Record for consultation research and training. *Journal of Educational and Psychological Consultation, 28*(4), 445–459. https://doi.org/10.1080/10474412.2017.1418366

Erchul, W. P., & Martens, B. K. (2010). *School consultation: Conceptual and empirical bases of practice*. Springer. https://doi.org/10.1007/978-1-4419-5747-4

Erchul, W. P., & Raven, B. H. (1997). Social power in school consultation: A contemporary view of French and Raven's bases of power model. *Journal of School Psychology, 35*(2), 137–171. https://doi.org/10.1016/S0022-4405(97)00002-2

Fagan, T. K. (1996). Witmer's contributions to school psychological services. *American Psychologist, 51*(3), 241–243. https://doi.org/10.1037/0003-066X.51.3.241

Fallon, L. M., Collier-Meek, M. A., Maggin, D. M., Sanetti, L. M. H., & Johnson, A. H. (2015). Is performance feedback for educators an evidence-based practice? A systematic review and evaluation based on single-case research. *Exceptional Children, 81*(2), 227–246. https://doi.org/10.1177/0014402914551738

Fauville, G., Luo, M., Queiroz, A. C. M., Bailenson, J. N., & Hancock, J. (2021). Nonverbal mechanisms predict Zoom fatigue and explain why women experience higher levels than men. *SSRN*. https://doi.org/10.2139/ssrn.3820035

Feldman, E. S., & Kratochwill, T. R. (2003). Problem solving consultation in schools: Past, present, and future directions. *The Behavior Analyst Today, 4*(3), 318–330. https://doi.org/10.1037/h0100022

Ferguson, J. L., Cihon, J. H., Leaf, J. B., Van Meter, S. M., McEachin, J., & Leaf, R. (2019). Assessment of social validity trends in the *Journal of Applied Behavior Analysis*. *European Journal of Behavior Analysis, 20*(1), 146–157. https://doi.org/10.1080/15021149.2018.1534771

Fischer, A. J., & Bloomfield, B. S. (2020). Using technology to maximize engagement and outcomes in family–school partnerships. In S. A. Garbacz (Ed.), *Establishing family–school partnerships in school psychology: Critical skills* (pp. 174–197). Routledge. https://doi.org/10.4324/9781138400382-9

Fischer, A. J., Bloomfield, B. S., Clark, R. R., McClelland, A. L., & Erchul, W. P. (2019). Increasing student compliance with teacher instructions using telepresence robot problem-solving teleconsultation. *International Journal of School & Educational Psychology, 7*(Suppl. 1), 158–172. https://doi.org/10.1080/21683603.2018.1470948

Fischer, A. J., Clark, R. R., Bloomfield, B. S., Askings, D. C., & Erchul, W. P. (2019). Using teleconsultation to teach expressive number discrimination through stimulus fading and reinforcement. *Journal of Applied School Psychology*, *35*(4), 339–356. https://doi.org/10.1080/15377903.2019.1587803

Fischer, A. J., Clark, R. R., & Lehman, E. (2018). Telepresence robotics and consultation. In A. J. Fischer, T. A. Collins, E. H. Dart, & K. C. Radley (Eds.), *Technology applications in school psychology consultation, supervision, and training* (pp. 62–82). Routledge. https://doi.org/10.4324/9781315175591-5

Fischer, A. J., Collier-Meek, M. A., Bloomfield, B., Erchul, W. P., & Gresham, F. M. (2017). A comparison of problem identification interviews conducted face-to-face and via videoconferencing using the consultation analysis record. *Journal of School Psychology*, *63*, 63–76. https://doi.org/10.1016/j.jsp.2017.03.009

Fischer, A. J., Collins, T. A., Dart, E. H., & Radley, K. C. (Eds.). (2019). *Technology applications in school psychology consultation, supervision, and training*. Routledge. https://doi.org/10.4324/9781315175591

Fischer, A. J., Dart, E. H., Leblanc, H., Hartman, K. L., Steeves, R. O., & Gresham, F. M. (2016). An investigation of the acceptability of videoconferencing within a school-based behavioral consultation framework: Demonstration of videoconferencing. *Psychology in the Schools*, *53*(3), 240–252. https://doi.org/10.1002/pits.21900

Fischer, A. J., Moy, G. E., Bloomfield, B. S., Whitcomb, S., & Florell, D. (2020). Faculty perceptions of distance education in school psychology training respecialization. *Trainers' Forum*, *37*(1), 34–43.

Fiske, K. E. (2008). Treatment integrity of school-based behavior analytic interventions: A review of the research. *Behavior Analysis in Practice*, *1*(2), 19–25. https://doi.org/10.1007/BF03391724

Florell, D. (2011). Using advancing technologies in the practice of school psychology. In T. M. Lionetti, E. P. Snyder, & R. W. Christner (Eds.), *A practical guide to building professional competencies in school psychology* (pp. 227–244). Springer. https://doi.org/10.1007/978-1-4419-6257-7_14

Fong, E. H., Catagnus, R. M., Brodhead, M. T., Quigley, S., & Field, S. (2016). Developing the cultural awareness skills of behavior analysts. *Behavior Analysis in Practice*, *9*(1), 84–94. https://doi.org/10.1007/s40617-016-0111-6

Fredricks, J. A., Blumenfeld, P. C., & Paris, A. H. (2004). School engagement: Potential of the concept, state of the evidence. *Review of Educational Research*, *74*(1), 59–109. https://doi.org/10.3102/00346543074001059

Frieder, J. E., Peterson, S. M., Woodward, J., Crane, J., & Garner, M. (2009). Teleconsultation in school settings: Linking classroom teachers and behavior analysts through web-based technology. *Behavior Analysis in Practice*, *2*(2), 32–39. https://doi.org/10.1007/BF03391746

Garbacz, S. A. (Ed.). (2020). *Establishing family–school partnerships in school psychology: Critical skills*. Routledge.

Gaztambide, D. J. (2012). Addressing cultural impasses with rupture resolution strategies: A proposal and recommendations. *Professional Psychology: Research and Practice, 43*(3), 183–189. https://doi.org/10.1037/a0026911

Gibson, J. L., Pennington, R. C., Stenhoff, D. M., & Hopper, J. S. (2010). Using desktop videoconferencing to deliver interventions to a preschool student with autism. *Topics in Early Childhood Special Education, 29*(4), 214–225. https://doi.org/10.1177/0271121409352873

Gilliard, C., & Culik, H. (2019). *Digital redlining, access, and privacy*. Common Sense Education. https://www.commonsense.org/education/articles/digital-redlining-access-and-privacy

Glover, T. A., Reddy, L. A., Kurz, A., & Elliott, S. N. (2019). Use of an online platform to facilitate and investigate data-driven instructional coaching. *Assessment for Effective Intervention, 44*(2), 95–103. https://doi.org/10.1177/1534508418811593

Greene, R. W., Abidin, R. R., & Kmetz, C. (1997). The index of teaching stress: A measure of student–teacher compatibility. *Journal of School Psychology, 35*(3), 239–259. https://doi.org/10.1016/S0022-4405(97)00006-X

Gresham, F. M. (2009). Evolution of the treatment integrity concept: Current status and future directions. *School Psychology Review, 38*(4), 533–540.

Groom, L. L., Brody, A. A., & Squires, A. P. (2021). Defining telepresence as experienced in telehealth encounters: A dimensional analysis. *Journal of Nursing Scholarship, 53*(6), 709–717. https://doi.org/10.1111/jnu.12684

Hagopian, L. P., Long, E. S., & Rush, K. S. (2004). Preference assessment procedures for individuals with developmental disabilities. *Behavior Modification, 28*(5), 668–677. https://doi.org/10.1177/0145445503259836

Hall, T. D. (2021). Information redlining: The urgency to close the digital access and literacy divide and the role of libraries as lead interveners. *Journal of Library Administration, 61*(4), 484–492. https://doi.org/10.1080/01930826.2021.1906559

Hanley, G. P. (2012). Functional assessment of problem behavior: Dispelling myths, overcoming implementation obstacles, and developing new lore. *Behavior Analysis in Practice, 5*(1), 54–72. https://doi.org/10.1007/BF03391818

Harvard University. (n.d.). *Pedagogical best practices: Residential, blended, and online*. Teach Remotely. https://teachremotely.harvard.edu/best-practices

Hawken, L. S. (2020). *Virtual check-in, check-out intervention* [Webinar]. University of Utah Technology in Training, Education, and Consultation (U-TTEC) Lab. https://www.youtube.com/watch?v=Hjq5u16Z6_s

Hawken, L. S., Crone, D. A., Bundock, K., & Horner, R. H. (2020). *Responding to problem behavior in schools: The check-in, check-out intervention* (3rd ed.). Guilford Press.

Health Insurance Portability and Accountability Act of 1996. Pub. L. 104–191. (1996)

Henrie, C. R., Halverson, L. R., & Graham, C. R. (2015). Measuring student engagement in technology-mediated learning: A review. *Computers & Education, 90*(1), 36–53. https://doi.org/10.1016/j.compedu.2015.09.005

Hilty, D. M., Sunderji, N., Suo, S., Chan, S., & McCarron, R. M. (2018). Telepsychiatry and other technologies for integrated care: Evidence base, best practice models and competencies. *International Review of Psychiatry, 30*(6), 292–309. https://doi.org/10.1080/09540261.2019.1571483

Hintze, J. M., Volpe, R. J., & Shapiro, E. S. (2002). Best practices in the systematic direct observation of student behavior. In A. Thomas & J. Grimes (Eds.), *Best practices in school psychology* (4th ed., pp. 993–1006). National Association of School Psychologists.

Howard, S. W., Mulligan Ault, M., Knowlton, H. E., & Swall, R. A. (1992). Distance education: Promises and cautions for special education. *Teacher Education and Special Education, 15*(4), 275–283. https://doi.org/10.1177/088840649201500406

Ikeda, M. J., Tucker, R., & Rankin, B. (2002). *Development, testing, and dissemination of nonaversive techniques for working with children with autism: Demonstration of a "best practices" model for parents and teachers. The A-B-C-D model for supporting students with autism (antecedents, behaviors, consequences, data). Final report.* https://eric.ed.gov/?id=ED472087

Imel, Z. E., Caperton, D. D., Tanana, M., & Atkins, D. C. (2017). Technology-enhanced human interaction in psychotherapy. *Journal of Counseling Psychology, 64*(4), 385–393. https://doi.org/10.1037/cou0000213

Individuals With Disabilities Education Act, 20 U.S.C. § 1400 (2004).

Jerome, L. W., & Zaylor, C. (2000). Cyberspace: Creating a therapeutic environment for telehealth applications. *Professional Psychology: Research and Practice, 31*(5), 478–483. https://doi.org/10.1037/0735-7028.31.5.478

Jimerson, S. R., Burns, M. K., & VanDerHeyden, A. M. (Eds.). (2016). *Handbook of response to intervention: The science and practice of multi-tiered systems of support* (2nd ed.). Springer. https://doi.org/10.1007/978-1-4899-7568-3

Kazdin, A. E., Holland, L., Crowley, M., & Breton, S. (1997). Barriers to Treatment Participation Scale: Evaluation and validation in the context of child outpatient treatment. *Journal of Child Psychology and Psychiatry, 38*, 1051–1062. https://doi.org/10.1111/j.1469-7610.1997.tb01621.x

Kennedy, C. H. (2002). The maintenance of behavior change as an indicator of social validity. *Behavior Modification, 26*(5), 594–604. https://doi.org/10.1177/014544502236652

Kent, R. N., O'Leary, K. D., Dietz, A., & Diament, C. (1979). Comparison of observational recordings in vivo, via mirror, and via television. *Journal of Applied Behavior Analysis, 12*(4), 517–522. https://doi.org/10.1901/jaba.1979.12-517

King, H. C., Bloomfield, B., Fischer, A. J., Dart, E., & Radley, K. (2020). A comparison of digital observations of students from video cameras and aerial drones.

Journal of Educational and Psychological Consultation, 31(3), 360–381. https://doi.org/10.1080/10474412.2020.1744446

King, H. C., Bloomfield, B. S., Wu, S., & Fischer, A. J. (2021). A systematic review of school teleconsultation: Implications for research and practice. *School Psychology Review, 51*(2), 237–256. https://doi.org/10.1080/2372966X.2021.1894478

King, H. C., Wu, S., Bloomfield, B. S., Fischer, A. J., & Martone, L. E. (2022). A practical guide on problem-solving teleconsultation in schools. *Journal of Educational and Psychological Consultation*. Advance online publication. https://doi.org/10.1080/10474412.2022.2070495

King, R., & Schindler, M. (2021, March 9). *A better path forward for criminal justice: Reconsidering police in schools*. Brookings. https://www.brookings.edu/research/a-better-path-forward-for-criminal-justice-reconsidering-police-in-schools/

Kirkpatrick, M., Akers, J., & Rivera, G. (2019). Use of behavioral skills training with teachers: A systematic review. *Journal of Behavioral Education, 28*(3), 344–361. https://doi.org/10.1007/s10864-019-09322-z

Korner, I. N., & Brown, W. H. (1952). The mechanical third ear. *Journal of Consulting Psychology, 16*(1), 81–84. https://doi.org/10.1037/h0061630

Kratochwill, T. R., & Bergan, J. R. (1990). *Behavioral consultation in applied settings*. Springer.

Kratochwill, T. R., Elliott, S. N., Loitz, P. A., Sladeczek, I., & Carlson, J. S. (2003). Conjoint consultation using self-administered manual and videotape parent-teacher training: Effects on children's behavioral difficulties. *School Psychology Quarterly, 18*(3), 269–302. https://doi.org/10.1521/scpq.18.3.269.22574

Kratochwill, T. R., Elliott, S. N., & Stoiber, K. C. (2002). Best practices in school-based problem solving consultation. In A. Thomas & J. Grimes (Eds.), *Best practices in school psychology* (4th ed., pp. 583–608). National Association of School Psychologists.

Lambert, N. M. (1974). A school-based consultation model. *Professional Psychology, 5*(3), 267–276. https://doi.org/10.1037/h0037311

Leach, M. J. (2005). Rapport: A key to treatment success. *Complementary Therapies in Clinical Practice, 11*(4), 262–265. https://doi.org/10.1016/j.ctcp.2005.05.005

Ledger, S., Burgess, M., Rappa, N., Power, B., Wong, K. W., Teo, T., & Hilliard, B. (2022). Simulation platforms in initial teacher education: Past practice informing future potentiality. *Computers & Education, 178*, Article 104385. https://doi.org/10.1016/j.compedu.2021.104385

Lorenzo-Lledó, A., Lledó, A., Gilabert-Cerdá, A., & Lorenzo, G. (2021). The pedagogical model of hybrid teaching: Difficulties of university students in the context of COVID-19. *European Journal of Investigation in Health, Psychology and Education, 11*(4), 1320–1332. https://doi.org/10.3390/ejihpe11040096

Louie, W., Korneder, J., Abbas, I., & Pawluk, C. (2020). A study on an applied behavior analysis-based robot-mediated listening comprehension intervention for ASD. *Paladyn, Journal of Behavioral Robotics, 12*(1), 31–46. https://doi.org/10.1515/pjbr-2021-0005

Lugo, A. M., King, M. L., Lamphere, J. C., & McArdle, P. E. (2017). Developing procedures to improve therapist–child rapport in early intervention. *Behavior Analysis in Practice, 10*(4), 395–401. https://doi.org/10.1007/s40617-016-0165-5

Machalicek, W., O'Reilly, M., Chan, J. M., Lang, R., Rispoli, M., Davis, T., Shogren, K., Sigafoos, J., Lancioni, G., Antonucci, M., Langthorne, P., Andrews, A., & Didden, R. (2009). Using videoconferencing to conduct functional analysis of challenging behavior and develop classroom behavioral support plans for students with autism. *Education and Training in Developmental Disabilities, 44*(2), 207–217.

Maheu, M. M., Drude, K. P., Hertlein, K. M., & Hilty, D. M. (2018). A framework of interprofessional telebehavioral health competencies: Implementation and challenges moving forward. *Academic Psychiatry, 42*(6), 825–833. https://doi.org/10.1007/s40596-018-0988-1

Makel, M. C., & Plucker, J. A. (2014). Facts are more important than novelty: Replication in the education sciences. *Educational Researcher, 43*(6), 304–316. https://doi.org/10.3102/0013189X14545513

Markelz, A. M., Taylor, J. C., Kitchen, T., Riccomini, P. J., Scheeler, M. C., & McNaughton, D. B. (2019). Effects of tactile prompting and self-monitoring on teachers' use of behavior-specific praise. *Exceptional Children, 85*(4), 471–489. https://doi.org/10.1177/0014402919846500

Martens, B. K., Witt, J. C., Elliott, S. N., & Darveaux, D. X. (1985). Teacher judgments concerning the acceptability of school-based interventions. *Professional Psychology: Research and Practice, 16*(2), 191–198. https://doi.org/10.1037/0735-7028.16.2.191

Martin, D. J., Garske, J. P., & Davis, M. K. (2000). Relation of the therapeutic alliance with outcome and other variables: A meta-analytic review. *Journal of Consulting and Clinical Psychology, 68*(3), 438–450. https://doi.org/10.1037/0022-006X.68.3.438

Maslach, C., & Jackson, S. E. (1981). *Maslach Burnout Inventory–ES Form (MBI)* [Database record]. APA PsycTests. https://doi.org/10.1037/t05190-000

Masland, M. C., Lou, C., & Snowden, L. (2010). Use of communication technologies to cost-effectively increase the availability of interpretation services in healthcare settings. *Telemedicine and e-Health, 16*(6), 739–745. https://doi.org/10.1089/tmj.2009.0186

McCullough, C. S., & Wenck, L. S. (1984). Current microcomputer applications in school psychology. *School Psychology Review, 13*(4), 429–439. https://doi.org/10.1080/02796015.1984.12085123

McDaniel, S. C., & Bloomfield, B. S. (2020). School-wide positive behavior support telecoaching in a rural district. *Journal of Educational Technology Systems, 48*(3), 335–355. https://doi.org/10.1177/0047239519886283

McDaniel, S. C., Bloomfield, B. S., Guyotte, K. W., Shannon, T. M., & Byrd, D. H. (2020). Telecoaching to support schoolwide positive behavior interventions and supports in rural schools. *Journal of Education for Students Placed at Risk, 26*(3), 236–252.

Meyers, J. (1973). A consultation model for school psychological services. *Journal of School Psychology, 11*(1), 5–15. https://doi.org/10.1016/0022-4405(73)90003-4

National Association of School Psychologists. (2020a). *Principles for professional ethics*. https://www.nasponline.org/standards-and-certification/professional-ethics

National Association of School Psychologists. (2020b). *Telehealth: Virtual service delivery updated recommendations*. https://www.nasponline.org/resources-and-publications/resources-and-podcasts/covid-19-resource-center/special-education-resources/telehealth-virtual-service-delivery-updated-recommendations

National Education Association. (2021). *Pedagogical practices in hybrid learning models*. https://www.nea.org/professional-excellence/student-engagement/tools-tips/pedagogical-practices-hybrid-learning-models

Nese, R. N. T., Meng, P., Breiner, S., Chaparro, E., & Algozzine, R. (2020). Using stakeholder feedback to improve online professional development opportunities. *Journal of Research on Technology in Education, 52*(2), 148–162. https://doi.org/10.1080/15391523.2020.1726233

Nock, M. K., & Photos, V. (2006). Parent motivation to participate in treatment: Assessment and prediction of subsequent participation. *Journal of Child and Family Studies, 15*(3), 333–346. https://doi.org/10.1007/s10826-006-9022-4

Nosik, M. R., & Carr, J. E. (2015). On the distinction between the motivating operation and setting event concepts. *The Behavior Analyst, 38*(2), 219–223. https://doi.org/10.1007/s40614-015-0042-5

Office for Civil Rights. (2021). *Notification of enforcement discretion for telehealth remote communications during the COVID-19 nationwide public health emergency*. U.S. Department of Health and Human Services. https://www.hhs.gov/hipaa/for-professionals/special-topics/emergency-preparedness/notification-enforcement-discretion-telehealth/index.html

O'Keeffe, S., Martin, P., & Midgley, N. (2020). When adolescents stop psychotherapy: Rupture–repair in the therapeutic alliance and association with therapy ending. *Psychotherapy, 57*(4), 471–490. https://doi.org/10.1037/pst0000279

O'Neill, R. E., Albin, R. W., Storey, K., Horner, R. H., & Sprague, J. R. (2015). *Functional assessment and program development for problem behavior: A practical handbook* (3rd ed.). Cengage Learning.

Open Science Collaboration. (2015). Estimating the reproducibility of psychological science. *Science, 349*(6251), Article 4716. https://doi.org/10.1126/science.aac4716

Paclawskyj, T. R., Matson, J. L., Rush, K. S., Smalls, Y., & Vollmer, T. R. (2000). Questions about behavioral function (QABF): A behavioral checklist for functional assessment of aberrant behavior. *Research in Developmental Disabilities*, *21*(3), 223–229. https://doi.org/10.1016/S0891-4222(00)00036-6

Pérez, J. Q., Daradoumis, T., & Puig, J. M. M. (2020). Rediscovering the use of chatbots in education: A systematic literature review. *Computer Applications in Engineering Education*, *28*(6), 1549–1565. https://doi.org/10.1002/cae.22326

Perrin, A. (2021, June 3). *Mobile technology and home broadband 2021*. Pew Research Center. https://www.pewresearch.org/internet/2021/06/03/mobile-technology-and-home-broadband-2021/

Peterson, S. M., Eldridge, R. R., Rios, D., & Schenk, Y. A. (2019). Ethical challenges encountered in delivering behavior analytic services through teleconsultation. *Behavior Analysis: Research and Practice*, *19*(2), 190–201. https://doi.org/10.1037/bar0000111

Plötz, T., Hammerla, N. Y., Rozga, A., Reavis, A., Call, N., & Abowd, G. D. (2012). Automatic assessment of problem behavior in individuals with developmental disabilities. *Proceedings of the 2012 Association for Computing Machinery Conference on Ubiquitous Computing*, 391–400. https://dl.acm.org/doi/10.1145/2370216.2370276

Radley, K. C., & Dart, E. H. (2019). Graphing data and visual analysis. In K. C. Radley & E. H. Dart (Eds.), *Handbook of behavioral interventions in schools: Multi-tiered systems of support* (pp. 71–88). Oxford University Press.

Radley, K. C., Dart, E. H., & O'Handley, R. D. (2016). The Quiet Classroom Game: A class-wide intervention to increase academic engagement and reduce disruptive behavior. *School Psychology Review*, *45*(1), 93–108. https://doi.org/10.17105/SPR45-1.93-108

Raes, A., Detienne, L., Windey, I., & Depaepe, F. (2019). A systematic literature review on synchronous hybrid learning: Gaps identified. *Learning Environments Research*, *23*(3), 269–290. https://doi.org/10.1007/s10984-019-09303-z

Renshaw, T. L., Long, A. C. J., & Cook, C. R. (2015). Assessing teachers' positive psychological functioning at work: Development and validation of the Teacher Subjective Wellbeing Questionnaire. *School Psychology Quarterly*, *30*(2), 289–306. https://doi.org/10.1037/spq0000112

Reschly, D. J. (1976). School psychology consultation: "Frenzied, faddish, or fundamental?" *Journal of School Psychology*, *14*(2), 105–113. https://doi.org/10.1016/0022-4405(76)90045-5

Rosenberg, N., & Huntington, R. N. (2021). Distance bug-in-ear coaching: A guide for practitioners. *Behavior Analysis in Practice*, *14*(2), 523–533. https://doi.org/10.1007/s40617-020-00534-8

Rousmaniere, T. (2014). Using technology to enhance clinical supervision and training. In C. E. Watkins & D. L. Milne (Eds.), *The Wiley international handbook of clinical supervision* (pp. 204–237). Wiley-Blackwell. https://doi.org/10.1002/9781118846360.ch9

Safran, J. D., Crocker, P., McMain, S., & Murray, P. (1990). Therapeutic alliance rupture as a therapy event for empirical investigation. *Psychotherapy: Theory, Research, & Practice, 27*(2), 154–165. https://doi.org/10.1037/0033-3204.27.2.154

Safran, J. D., & Muran, J. C. (1996). The resolution of ruptures in the therapeutic alliance. *Journal of Consulting and Clinical Psychology, 64*(3), 447–458. https://doi.org/10.1037/0022-006X.64.3.447

Safran, J. D., Muran, J. C., & Eubanks-Carter, C. (2011). Repairing alliance ruptures. *Psychotherapy, 48*(1), 80–87. https://doi.org/10.1037/a0022140

Sanetti, L. M. H., & Collier-Meek, M. A. (2014). Increasing the rigor of procedural fidelity assessment: An empirical comparison of direct observation and permanent product review methods. *Journal of Behavioral Education, 23*(1), 60–88. https://doi.org/10.1007/s10864-013-9179-z

Sanetti, L. M. H., & Collier-Meek, M. A. (2017). Treatment integrity: Evidence-based interventions in applied settings. In L. A. Theodore (Ed.), *Handbook of evidence-based interventions for children and adolescents* (pp. 3–14). Springer.

Sanetti, L. M. H., & Collier-Meek, M. A. (2019). *Supporting successful interventions in schools: Tools to plan, evaluate, and sustain effective implementation.* Guilford Press.

Scheeler, M. C., & Lee, D. L. (2002). Using technology to deliver immediate corrective feedback to preservice teachers. *Journal of Behavioral Education, 11*(4), 231–241. https://doi.org/10.1023/A:1021158805714

Schultz, B. K., Zoder-Martell, K. A., Fischer, A., Collier-Meek, M. A., Erchul, W. P., & Schoemann, A. M. (2018). When is teleconsultation acceptable to school psychologists? *Journal of Educational and Psychological Consultation, 28*(3), 279–296. https://doi.org/10.1080/10474412.2017.1385397

Schwartz, I. S., & Baer, D. M. (1991). Social validity assessments: Is current practice state of the art? *Journal of Applied Behavior Analysis, 24*(2), 189–204. https://doi.org/10.1901/jaba.1991.24-189

Sellers, T., & Walker, S. (2019). Telesupervision. In A. J. Fischer, T. A. Collins, E. H. Dart, & K. C. Radley (Eds.), *Technology applications in school psychology consultation, supervision, and training* (106–126). https://doi.org/10.4324/9781315175591

Sheridan, S. M., Kratochwill, T. R., & Bergan, J. R. (1996). *Conjoint behavioral consultation: A procedural manual.* Plenum. https://doi.org/10.1007/978-1-4757-2512-4

Sheridan, S. M., Kratochwill, T. R., & Burt, J. D. (2008). *Conjoint behavioral consultation: Promoting family–school connections and interventions* (2nd ed.). Springer.

Sheridan, S. M., Welch, M., & Orme, S. F. (1996). Is consultation effective? A review of outcome research. *Remedial and Special Education, 17*(6), 341–354. https://doi.org/10.1177/074193259601700605

Silver, L. (2019). *Smartphone ownership is growing rapidly around the world, but not always equally*. Pew Research Center. https://www.pewresearch.org/global/2019/02/05/smartphone-ownership-is-growing-rapidly-around-the-world-but-not-always-equally/

Stamm, B. H. (2009). *Professional quality of life: Compassion satisfaction and fatigue subscales, Version V (ProQOL)*. Center for Victims of Torture. https://proqol.org/ProQol_Test.html

Steege, M. W., Pratt, J. L., Wickerd, G., Guare, R., & Watson, T. S. (2019). *Conducting school-based functional behavioral assessments: A practitioner's guide*. Guilford Press.

Stormont, M. (Ed.). (2012). *Academic and behavior supports for at-risk students: Tier 2 interventions*. Guilford Press.

Stowitschek, J. J., Mangus, B., & Rule, S. (1986). Inservice training via telecommunications: Out of the workshop and into the classroom. *Educational Technology, 26*(8), 28–33.

Sutherland, K. S., Wheby, J. H., & Yoder, P. J. (2002). Examination of the relationship between teacher praise and opportunities for students with EBD to respond to academic requests. *Journal of Emotional and Behavioral Disorders, 10*(1), 5–13. https://doi.org/10.1177/106342660201000102

Tanana, M. J., Soma, C. S., Srikumar, V., Atkins, D. C., & Imel, Z. E. (2019). Development and evaluation of ClientBot: Patient-like conversational agent to train basic counseling skills. *Journal of Medical Internet Research, 21*(7), Article e12529. https://doi.org/10.2196/12529

Taylor, B. A., LeBlanc, L. A., & Nosik, M. (2019). Compassionate care in behavior analytic treatment: Can outcomes be enhanced by attending to relationships with caregivers? *Behavior Analysis in Practice*. Advance online publication. https://doi.org/10.1007/s40617-018-00289-3

Tiger, J. H., Hanley, G. P., & Bruzek, J. (2008). Functional communication training: A review and practical guide. *Behavior Analysis in Practice, 1*(1), 16–23. https://doi.org/10.1007/BF03391716

Wahler, R. G., & Fox, J. J. (1981). Setting events in applied behavior analysis: Toward a conceptual and methodological expansion. *Journal of Applied Behavior Analysis, 14*(3), 327–338. https://doi.org/10.1901/jaba.1981.14-327

Warren, J. M. (2018). *School consultation for student success: A cognitive-behavioral approach*. Springer.

Webster-Stratton, C. (1981). Videotape modeling: A method of parent education. *Journal of Clinical Child Psychology, 10*(2), 93–98. https://doi.org/10.1080/15374418109533023

Webster-Stratton, C., Kolpacoff, M., & Hollinsworth, T. (1988). Self-administered videotape therapy for families with conduct-problem children: Comparison with two cost-effective treatments and a control group. *Journal of Consulting and Clinical Psychology, 56*(4), 558–566. https://doi.org/10.1037/0022-006X.56.4.558

White, K. R., Radley, K. C., Olmi, D. J., & McKinley, L. E. (2022). Increasing teachers' use of behavior specific praise via Apple Watch prompting. *Psychology in the Schools, 59*(3), 480–494. https://doi.org/10.1002/pits.22622

Witt, J. C., & Elliott, S. N. (1985). Acceptability of classroom management strategies. In T. R. Kratochwill (Ed.), *Advances in school psychology* (Vol. 4, pp. 251–288). Lawrence Erlbaum.

Wolf, M. M. (1978). Social validity: The case for subjective measurement or how applied behavior analysis is finding its heart. *Journal of Applied Behavior Analysis, 11*(2), 203–214. https://doi.org/10.1901/jaba.1978.11-203

Zoder-Martell, K., Dufrene, B., Sterling, H., Tingstrom, D., Blaze, J., Duncan, N., & Harpole, L. (2013). Effects of verbal and graphed feedback on treatment integrity. *Journal of Applied School Psychology, 29*(4), 328–349. https://doi.org/10.1080/15377903.2013.836776

Zoder-Martell, K. A., Markelz, A. M., Floress, M. T., Skriba, H. A., & Sayyah, L. E. N. (2020). Technology to facilitate telehealth in applied behavior analysis. *Behavior Analysis in Practice, 13*(3), 596–603. https://doi.org/10.1007/s40617-020-00449-4s

Index

A

ABC Data Collection Checklist, 77
ABC (antecedent–behavior–consequence) model, 74–76, 88–89
Accessibility of services, 149
Administrative consultations, 10
Aerial drones, 151–152
AI (artificial intelligence), 153–154
American Academy of Child and Adolescent Psychiatry, 142–143
American Psychological Association (APA), 23–24
Antecedent–behavior–consequence (ABC) model, 74–76, 88–89
Applications
 asynchronous, 4, 7, 153–156
 research on, 157–160
 synchronous, 3, 6, 15, 149–153
 training, 156–157
AR (augmented reality), 7, 156–157
Artificial intelligence (AI), 153–154. *See also* Machine learning
Asynchronous applications, 4, 7, 153–156
Asynchronous feedback, 114–115
Attention function, strategies associated with, 105
Audio feedback, 13–14
Audio feeds, 95
Audio quality, 47
Augmented reality (AR), 7, 156–157
Avoidance, session, 63

B

BAA (business associate agreement), 29
BACB (Behavior Analyst Certification Board), 23–24
Bandwidth, 137
Bar graphs, 89–90
Barretto, A., 17
Barriers, 135–146
 behavior- and crisis-related, 141–142
 child care-related, 142–143
 computing and technical, 138–140
 with hybrid delivery model, 143–144
 planning and organizational, 140–141
 privacy- and security-related, 144–145
 and social validity, 145–146
 systemic, 136–137
 travel-related, 142
Barriers to Treatment Participation Scale, 114
Behavior(s)
 antecedents of, 74
 assessments of, 18
 barriers related to, 141–142
 consequences of, 74
 definition, 73
 function of, 91
 maintenance of changed, 158
Behavioral consultation model, 11
Behavioral functions, 105
Behavioral Response Support Team, 109
Behavioral skills training (BST), 25–26, 108
Behavior Analyst Certification Board (BACB), 23–24

175

Behavior Intervention Rating Scale, 122
Belar, C. D., 15
BITE (bug-in-the-ear) technology, 14, 19
Bloomfield, B. S., 19, 108
Boundaries, setting, 53
Brown, J. M., 45–46
Brown, W. H., 14
BST (behavioral skills training), 108
Bug-in-the-ear (BITE) technology, 14, 19
Business associate agreement (BAA), 29

C

Cameras, 95, 150
Cancellations, 63, 65
Caplan, G., 10
Caregivers, rapport with, 51
Case consultations, consultee-centered, 10
CD-ROMs, 15
Child care-related barriers, 142–143
Classroom context, 54
Clopton, K. L., 17
Cloud-based storage, 7
Coaching, ongoing, 125
Coalition for Technology in Behavioral Science, 60
Committee on Health Care Access, 142–143
Communication(s)
  effective, 52
  nonverbal, 57, 64–65
  setting boundaries around, 53
  written, 155
Competence, 25–27
Computing barriers, 138–139
Confidentiality, 24–25
Consent process, 24, 94–95
Consultant Evaluation Form, 66, 122
Consultee(s), 6
  follow-up, 50
  implementation support, 114
  interests of, 54
  learning and development, intersectional support of, 45
  no-show, 63, 65
Consultee-centered consultations, 10
Contextualization, 57
Contextual variables, of behavior, 74
Counseling the counselors model, 10
COVID-19 pandemic, 29–30, 143
Crisis plan, 107–108

Crisis-related barriers, 141–142
Cultural diversity, 45

D

Darian (fictional case subject). *See* Schoolwide teleconsultation referral (fictional case)
Dart, E. H., 106
Data
  collection of, 75, 77, 92
  review of, 89–91
Department of Health and Human Services (DHHS), 29
Devices, wearable, 152
Dial-up internet, 15
Digital redlining, 149
Dignity, respect for, 24–25
Direct services, 11
Distance education, 15–16
Diversity, 45–46, 157
Documentation, 26
Drones, 151–152

E

Economics Task Force on Mental Health, 142–143
Education, distance, 15–16
Educators, rapport with, 51
Educator-targeted direct services, 11
Emails, 25
Engagement, in teleconsultation, 57
Erchul, W. P., 35, 156
Escape function, strategies associated with, 105
Estella (fictional case subject). *See* Intensive needs teleconsultation (fictional case)
Ethical issues. *See* Professional and ethical issues
Ethical Principles of Psychologists and Code of Conduct (APA), 23–24
Expectations, for consultations, 55

F

Face-to-face (term), 7
Family-school partnerships, 158
FBA (functional behavior assessment), 78–81

Feedback
asynchronous, 114–115
audio, 13–14
initial performance, 110–112
ongoing performance, 125–126
openness to, 52
Fiber-optic connections, 15
Fischer, A. J., 20, 154
Flip (software), 155
Follow-up, 61–62
Frieder, J. E., 18
Functional analysis, 94–96
Functional behavior assessment (FBA), 78–81
Future of School Psychology conference, 16
Future research, directions for, 147–160
asynchronous applications, 153–156
research applications, 157–160
synchronous applications, 149–153
training applications, 156–157

G

Garbacz, S. A., 35
Gender diversity, 45
Gibson, J. L., 18
GoReact (software), 155
Granite School District, 109
Graphs, bar and line, 89–90
Groom, L. L., 48

H

Hardware access, 136–137
Headphones, 95–96
History of teleconsultation, 9–21
acceptability and practicality of, 20–21
early, 12–17
in schools, 17–20
Honesty, 27–28
Hybrid applications, 4
Hybrid delivery model barriers, 143–144

I

Inclusive teleconsultation, 44–46
Index of Teaching Stress, 122
Indirect service to the child, 11
Individuals With Disabilities Education Act (2004), 78
Inequities, in accessibility of services, 149
Initial performance feedback, 110–112

Initiation of communication, 50
In-person service provision, 7
Integrity, 27–28
Intensive needs teleconsultation (fictional case)
building rapport in, 68–69
evaluation of, 129–130
intervention planning, training, and support of, 117–119
introduction to, 39–41
problem analysis of, 98–101
problem identification in, 84–85
Intentionality, 51–52
Internet access, 137
Interpersonal considerations, in rapport-building, 62–66
Interpretation services, 152–153
Interruptions, limiting, 62–63, 65
Intersectionality, 45
Intervention materials preparation, 107
Intervention planning, training, and support, 103–119
after training and implementation sessions, 113
intensive needs teleconsultation (fictional case), 117–119
in intervention implementation session, 111–113
intervention plans, 91–92
before intervention training session, 104–108
in intervention training session, 108–111
problem solving during plan implementation, 113–115
schoolwide teleconsultation referral (fictional case), 116–117
social validity, 115–116
Intervention Rating Profile (IRP), 115, 122

K

Kent, R. N., 13
King, H. C, 18, 151, 157
Kirkpatrick, M., 108
Knesting, K., 17
Korner, L. N., 14
Kratochwill, T. R., 14, 35

L

Language, approachable, 52–53
Levels of support, in school consultations, 5

178 • Index

Lighting considerations, 47–48
Line graphs, 89–90
Lyssn (software), 155

M

Machalicek, W., 18
Machine learning, 154–155
Maheu, M. M., 46, 54
Maslach Burnout Inventory, 122
McDaniel, S. C., 19
Mental health consultation, 10
Meyers, J., 11
Meyers' four-level model, 11
Microcomputers, 13
Motivating operations, 74
Motivation, 60–61
Multicomponent plans, 127–128
Mursion (software), 156
Mutual respect, 53

N

National Association of School Psychologists (NASP), 23–24
National Education Association (NEA), 144
Nico (fictional case subject). *See* Intensive needs teleconsultation (fictional case)
Nonverbal communication, 57, 64–65
No-shows, 63, 65

O

Observations, systematic direct, 75–76
Office for Civil Rights, 29
Ongoing coaching, 125
Online (term), 7
Online companion materials, 6
Online learning, 159–160
Opportunities to respond, 58
Optimization of teleconsultation, 47
Organizational consultation, 11

P

PAI. *See* Problem analysis interview
Parenting Stress Index, 122
Parent Motivation Inventory, 114
Participant demographics, 157
Performance feedback, ongoing, 125–126
Permanent products, 75–76
Pew Research Center, 29

PII. *See* Problem identification interview
Plan evaluation, 37
Planning and organizational barriers, 140–141
Plan training and implementation, 37
Positionality, 54–55
Postsession rapport, 59–62
Power imbalances, 45–46
Practice, research vs. applied, 148
Preference assessments, 18
Presence and engagement, in rapport-building, 48–50
Principles for Professional Ethics (NASP), 23–24
Privacy, 24–25, 144–145
Problem analysis, as stage in problem-solving teleconsultation, 36
Problem analysis interview (PAI), 87–101
 intensive needs teleconsultation (fictional case), 98–101
 postinterview actions, 92–93
 preinterview actions, 88–89
 problem solving during, 93–96
 schoolwide teleconsultation referral (fictional case), 96–97
 social validity during, 93–96
 steps during, 89–92
Problem identification, as stage in problem-solving teleconsultation, 36
Problem identification interview (PII), 71–85
 functional behavior assessment, 78–81
 intensive needs teleconsultation (fictional case), 84–85
 postinterview actions, 77–78
 preinterview actions, 72
 problem solving during, 81–82
 schoolwide teleconsultation referral (fictional case), 82–84
 social validity during, 82
 steps during, 73–77
Problem solving
 consultation, 11
 in problem analysis stage, 93–96
 in problem evaluation stage, 127–128
 in problem identification stage, 81–82
 teleconsultation framework, 35–37
Process and outcomes evaluation, 121–130
 intensive needs teleconsultation (fictional case), 129–130
 in plan evaluation process, 123–125
 postsession actions, 125–127

presession actions, 121–123
problem solving during problem evaluation stage, 127–128
schoolwide teleconsultation referral (fictional case), 128–129
social validity during problem evaluation stage, 128
Products, permanent, 75–76
Professional and ethical issues, 23–31
   access to teleconsultation, 30–31
   challenges in, 28–29
   competence and responsibility, 25–27
   decision making in, 29–30
   honesty and integrity, 27–28
   professional responsibilities, 28
   respect for dignity, 24–25
Professional Quality of Life Scale, 122
Program-centered administrative consultation, 10
Progress monitoring, 26, 75

Q

Questions, openness for, 52

R

Racial minorities, 45
Raes, A., 144
Rapport building, 43–69
   after sessions, 59–62
   initiation of communication, 50
   intensive needs teleconsultation (fictional case), 68–69
   interpersonal considerations, 62–66
   presence and engagement, 48–50
   prior to sessions, 44–48
   ruptures and repair of rapport, 63–65
   schoolwide teleconsultation referral (fictional case), 66–68
   slow development, 63, 65
   as stage in problem-solving teleconsultation, 36
   strategies and tools for, 58
   in virtual face-to-face sessions, 51–59
Ratings, direct behavior, 75–76
Redlining, digital, 149
Relationship building. *See* Rapport building
Replication crisis, 148
Research, applied practice vs., 148
Research applications, 157–160
Respect, mutual, 53

Responsibilities
   allocation of, 56
   professional, 25–28
Robots, telepresence, 7, 19, 150–151
Roles, establishing, 55
Ruptured rapport, 63–64

S

Safety plan, 107–108
SARs (socially assistive robots), 157
Satellite communications, 15
Scatterplots, 75–76
School context, 54
School psychological consultation, Meyers' four-level model of, 11
School psychologists, 9
School Psychology Review, 13
School teleconsultation, 6
School-Wide Positive Behavioral Interventions and Supports (SW-PBIS), 19–20
Schoolwide teleconsultation referral (fictional case)
   building rapport in, 66–68
   evaluation of, 128–129
   intervention planning, training, and support of, 116–117
   introduction to, 38–39
   problem analysis of, 96–97
   problem identification in, 82–84
Schultz, B. K., 21
Security-related barriers, 144–145
Self-efficacy, 122
Service to the school system, 11
Session avoidance, 63
Session cancellations, 63, 65
Setting events, 74–75
Sexual diversity, 45
Shared trust, 53
Sheridan, S. M., 35
Skills
   discussion of, 108–109
   modeling of, 109, 113–114
   rehearsal of, 110
Social influence, 43
Socially assistive robots (SARs), 157
Social media, 27
Social validity, 64–66
   and barriers to teleconsultation, 145–146
   in intervention planning/training/support stage, 115–116

in problem analysis stage, 93–96
in problem evaluation stage, 128
in problem identification stage, 82
Social validity, assessment of, 122
Software access, 136–137
Stowitschek, J. J., 16
Student-centered case consultation, 10
Student context, reassessment of, 127
Students
   characteristics of, 73
   rapport with, 56–59
   as term, 6
Student-targeted direct services, 11
SW-PBIS (School-Wide Positive Behavioral Interventions and Supports), 19–20
Synchronous applications, 3, 6, 15, 149–153
Systemic barriers, 136–137

T

Tangible function, strategies associated with, 105
Targeted teleconsultation sessions, 49
Taylor, B. A., 64
Teachers, rapport with, 51
Teacher Subjective Wellbeing Questionnaire, 122
Teacher-targeted direct services, 11
TeachLivE, 156
Technical barriers, 139–140
Technologies, wearable, 152
Technology Acceptance Model–Fast Form, 122
Technology habituation, 93–94
Telecommunication technologies, 6
Teleconsultation. *See also* History of teleconsultation
   challenges of, 19
   environment of, 46–47
   goals of, 124–125
   inclusive, 44–46
   limits of, 158
   process of, 4
   session length for, 49

Telehealth, 3, 6
Telepresence, 48
Telepresence robots, 7, 19, 150–151
Telesupervision, 155
Training applications, 156–157
Travel-related barriers, 142
Treatment integrity, 111

U

University of Utah, 109

V

Video
   observation via, 13
   quality of, 47–48
Video capturing devices, 149–150
Videoconferencing, 7, 16–17, 50
Video feeds, 95
Video modeling, 14–15
Virtual assistants, 153
Virtual backgrounds, 49
Virtual face-to-face sessions, rapport-building in, 51–59
Virtual reality (VR), 7, 156–157
Vyond (software), 109

W

Wearable devices, 152
Webcams, 47–48
Webster-Stratton, C., 14
Wendy (fictional case subject). *See* Intensive needs teleconsultation (fictional case)
Witmer, L., 9

Z

Zoe (fictional case subject). *See* School-wide teleconsultation referral (fictional case)
Zoom, 137

About the Authors

Aaron J. Fischer, PhD, BCBA-D, is an associate professor of school psychology in the Department of Educational Psychology and an adjunct associate professor of Psychiatry at the University of Utah. He conducts technology-focused research in educational and psychological settings, specifically using telepresence robotics with teachers during school and clinic-based consultation. His current research emphasizes the integration of cutting-edge technology in school and psychological practice. Dr. Fischer is coeditor of two related texts, *Computer-Assisted and Web-Based Innovations in Psychology, Special Education, and Health* and *Technology Applications in School Psychology Consultation, Supervision, and Training*.

Bradley S. Bloomfield, PhD, BCBA-D, CBA, is a senior lecturer in applied behaviour analysis at Monash University. He conducts research in teleconsultation to support parents and teachers, and evidence-based behavior interventions. His research agenda is to increase inclusion for young people whose challenging behavior inhibits their access to the community by focusing on the application of consultation models to support educators, families, and service providers to implement high-quality evidence-based behavior interventions. His work has resulted in numerous invitations for contributions to presentations, workshops, peer reviews, podcasts, and interviews with media outlets internationally.